AN ILLUSTRATED GUIDE TO
FRIGATES OF THE WORLD

AN ILLUSTRATED GUIDE TO
FRIGATES OF THE WORLD

A history of over 70 classes with 235 identification photographs

A country-by-country directory of ships, including the Flowers, Floréals, Garcias, Minervas, Kolas, Sachsens, and many more

Bernard Ireland

southwater

This edition is published by Southwater
an imprint of Anness Publishing Ltd
Blaby Road
Wigston
Leicestershire LE18 4SE
info@anness.com

www.southwaterbooks.com
www.annesspublishing.com

Anness Publishing has a new picture agency
outlet for images for publishing, promotions
or advertising. Please visit our website
www.practicalpictures.com for more information.

Publisher: Joanna Lorenz
Senior Editor: Felicity Forster
Copy Editor: Will Fowler
Cover Design: Nigel Partridge
Designer: Design Principals
Production Controller: Bessie Bai

PUBLISHER'S NOTES
Although the information in this book is believed to be accurate
and true at the time of going to press, neither the authors nor the
publisher can accept any legal responsibility or liability for any errors
or omissions that may be made.
    The nationality of each ship is identified in the specification
box by the national flag that was in use at the time of the vessel's
commissioning and service.

PAGE 1: *Braunschweig*, Braunschweig class.
PAGE 2: *Surcouf*, La Fayette class.
PAGE 3: *Algonquin*, Iroquois class.
BELOW: *Scarborough*, Type 12 class.

ETHICAL TRADING POLICY
At Anness Publishing we believe that business should be conducted
in an ethical and ecologically sustainable way, with respect for the
environment and a proper regard to the replacement of the natural
resources we employ.

As a publisher, we use a lot of wood pulp in high-quality paper
for printing, and that wood commonly comes from spruce trees.
We are therefore currently growing more than 750,000 trees in three
Scottish forest plantations: Berrymoss (130 hectares/320 acres),
West Touxhill (125 hectares/305 acres) and Deveron Forest
(75 hectares/185 acres). The forests we manage contain more
than 3.5 times the number of trees employed each year in making
paper for the books we manufacture.

Because of this ongoing ecological investment programme, you,
as our customer, can have the pleasure and reassurance of knowing
that a tree is being cultivated on your behalf to naturally replace the
materials used to make the book you are holding.

Our forestry programme is run in accordance with the UK Woodland
Assurance Scheme (UKWAS) and will be certified by the internationally
recognized Forest Stewardship Council (FSC). The FSC is a
non-government organization dedicated to promoting responsible
management of the world's forests. Certification ensures forests
are managed in an environmentally sustainable and socially
responsible way. For further information about this scheme,
go to www.annesspublishing.com/trees.

Previously published as part of a larger volume,
The World Encyclopedia of Destroyers and Frigates

ACKNOWLEDGEMENTS
Research for the images used to illustrate this book was carried
out by Ted Nevill of Cody Images, who supplied the majority of
pictures. The publisher and Ted Nevill would like to thank all those
who contributed to this research and to the supply of pictures:
AgustaWestland; ArtTech; BAE SYSTEMS; Blohm & Voss; General
Dynamics; Japanese Maritime Self-Defense Force; Koninklijke
Marine (Royal Netherlands Navy); Marina Militare, Republica Italiana
(Italian Navy); NATO; Naval Historical Center, USA; National Archives
& Records Administration, USA; Thomas Reyer; Ulis Fleming;
US Naval Institute; US Navy; US Department of Defense.

Contents

Introduction

If a single word summed up the sailing frigate, it would be versatility. Almost invariably with a single gun deck, she was not powerful enough to lay in a line of battle, but had sailing qualities superior to those of heavier ships. Often permitted to cruise, or act independently, frigates were popular commands, and the nemesis of privateers that preyed on commercial shipping. They also assumed the drudgery of escorting slow, ill-disciplined convoys. Their supreme quality was their speed, useful not only in reconnaissance but also in close blockade, loitering on an enemy's doorstep to give an early warning of every sortie.

Corvettes were smaller, invariably flush-decked and often with a largely open gun deck. Never a precise term in the Royal Navy, "corvette" referred generally to vessels smaller than a frigate but larger than a ship sloop. With the technological advances of the latter 19th century, both frigate and corvette died terminological deaths.

The submarine campaign of World War I saw the rehabilitation of the sloop as a specialist escort deploying the rudimentary sensors and weapons then current. Post-war, acute shortage of funds slowed, even crippled, promising lines of development, including ahead-throwing weapons. Progress during the 1930s was, however, necessarily accelerated as

ABOVE: **Rapid escalation in size and cost during the 1950s resulted in the British experimenting with a "utility" frigate. The Type 14 (*Hardy* shown here) had the anti-submarine (AS) firepower of a Type 12 on the smallest practicable single-screw hull.**

a repeat submarine threat evolved. By the lead-up to World War II, the British Admiralty thus had in production Black Swan-class sloops for ocean convoy escort, and Flower-class corvettes for equivalent coastal duties. The sloops (defying historical precedent by being larger and more capable than the corvettes) were excellent ships, but too expensive to be built in the numbers required. Scores of yards in Britain and abroad, particularly in Canada, were able to build the 200ft Flowers which, *faut de mieux*, were used deep-sea, where their modest speed, range and habitability were all too evident.

The Flowers' shortcomings were immediately addressed in the twin-screw corvette, which entered service under the resurrected generic name of frigate. These, the Rivers, had the length to cope with Atlantic conditions and, importantly, were both faster and more capacious. Only then was it being realized by just what degree the efficiency of even the best crews was reduced by the relentlessly fierce motion of small ships.

LEFT: **World War II depth charge crews in action. The economically based pre-war decision not to progress and develop an effective ahead-throwing weapon was a misjudgement of considerable magnitude, delaying the defeat of the U-boat by at least a year.** ABOVE: **The 300ft destroyer escort was the American equivalent to the frigate. In a programme of staggering dimensions, over 1,000 hulls were ordered, of which nearly 500 were completed to six standard specifications.** BELOW: **To increase numbers, the British Type 22s (Brazen shown here) were designed to a budget. The result was over-tight and unsatisfactory, with later ships having to be considerably stretched.** BOTTOM: **Current destroyers and frigates are dominated by measures designed to reduce radar reflection. The German Hessen is designed along MEKO (MEhrzweck KOmbination or, roughly, multi-purpose) principles to allow systems to be more easily interchanged or upgraded.**

This early story is very much one of British experience as it was they, faced again with a U-boat onslaught, who made the running in the development of anti-submarine (AS) ships.

Post-war, the realignment of national blocs saw the creation of NATO and a broad standardization of terminology. Thus, the category of frigate now embraced all types of capable AS vessels. Once again, sloops and corvettes passed into obsolescence.

"Fast" frigates were to prove inadequate against the always-faster submarine, resulting firstly in stand-off weapons, and then the organic helicopter. Two helicopters proved to be more effective than one.

It is accepted wisdom in warship design that successive, "improved" classes increase in size. So it has been with the frigate, which is gradually assuming the parallel characteristics of the destroyer. As has happened in the past, the sheer cost of such super-specimens has created a niche market for smaller, simpler craft. The wheel has again turned and, once more, the corvette is alive and well.

This book opens with a series of topics detailing development in frigate design and illustrating the use of frigates in action. Following this is a directory of over 70 significant classes, each entry comprising a description, one or more photographs and a data panel, standardized to permit direct comparisons to be made. Sheer numbers require that individual ship names are listed in a single section toward the end of the book, where a useful glossary of naval terms may also be found.

A History of Frigates

The major threat to trade during the sailing era was from privateers, frigates being called upon both to counter such raiders and to escort convoys. With World War I, commercial shipping was faced with the greater menace of the U-boat. Although convoys were re-introduced and specialist anti-submarine (AS) sloops made their appearance, the threat was not overcome by 1918.

Tight inter-war budgets saw AS warfare neglected, but by 1939 the British Admiralty had developed a new AS sloop for ocean convoy escort, and a corvette as its coastal equivalent. Experience proved the sloop too expensive and complex for volume production, and the corvette too limited to take its place. A larger "twin-screw corvette" was introduced, entering service under the re-instated designation of "frigate". Married to new ahead-firing weapons, it was an efficient U-boat killer. The post-war creation of NATO saw the "frigate" category extended to include all capable AS ships.

To counter the fast submarine, increased ship speeds proved ineffective, and frigate sizes escalated with the adoption of stand-off missiles, then helicopters. Relentless cost increases have thus seen the re-introduction of the "corvette" as a cheaper "low-end" substitute.

LEFT: **First of class, a pristine *Oliver Hazard Perry* sails for builders' trials. The single-arm Standard/Harpoon launcher was later removed as the ships assumed more general duties, with fleet numbers shrinking.**

The submarine threat in 1939

Still, more correctly, a submersible, the submarine of 1939 spent most of its time on the surface. Conserving both power and air, it might remain submerged for 24 hours or more but would then be obliged to surface to recharge its batteries and its internal atmosphere.

Submarines were slow compared with surface ships, even though the latter were subject to weather conditions. For instance, the German Type VIIC boat, workhorse of the U-boat fleet, could make 17 knots on the surface (half the speed of a destroyer) but only 7½ knots submerged. Restraining her submerged speed to just 4 knots (a smart walking pace) she could travel a maximum of 128km/80 miles. It followed that a submerged submarine could not escape an escort by flight, only by stealth.

A further limitation of a VIIC was that she could carry only 14 torpedoes. As "spreads" were frequently launched to guarantee a hit, these could be quickly exhausted. A U-boat thus had to be resupplied at sea or spend most of her time on passage. A network of ocean re-supply ships was thus established, and these could be targeted.

To offset all these shortcomings, the submarine retained the enormous advantage of invisibility. While she could not

> "We have got to the stage when the hitherto 'undetectable craft' is detectable ... the time is coming when we shall have to re–balance our theories as to the tactical use of submarines."
> Minute by Rear Admiral Chatfield, Assistant Chief of Naval Staff, July 1921, following Asdic trials

TOP: **A sight to stir any destroyerman's heart. Destroyers, however, were designed for fleet screening and proved to be deficient submarine hunters, being short-legged and with insufficient accommodation, particularly for equipment.** ABOVE: **Woefully unprepared for submarine warfare, the Americans seemed powerless to prevent a handful of Dönitz's U-boats creating mayhem off the eastern seaboard early in 1942. Here, the tanker *Dixie Arrow* burns herself out.**

be seen, she could, however, be heard. Machinery, propeller cavitation and water flow over the hull's many excrescences could, in quiet conditions, be detected on a sensitive hydrophone, the only method available during World War I. The sea, however, is never quiet, while the vessel carrying the hydrophone would, herself, generate noise. Work was already in progress in Great Britain, the United States and France to build an oscillator that would produce pulses of acoustic energy. These, transmitted through the water, would result in some of the energy being reflected from a solid body, such as a submarine. The reflected pulse would be detected by a hull-mounted hydrophone.

LEFT: By 1945, the chance of a depth charge attack being successful had increased from five to seven per cent. Hedgehog, however, subject to less "dead time" eventually improved to about 30 per cent. Squid was even better, but arrived too late to affect the outcome. ABOVE: The 1930s-trained U-boat skippers were resourceful and dedicated. They enjoyed their initial "Happy Time" but, once they had been accounted for, their replacements deteriorated in quality as that of Allied escort commanders improved.

Refinement of the system took time and the first production sets of what was termed Asdic (later Sonar) appeared in fleet destroyers only in the early 1930s. Acoustic transmission in the sea column is capricious but Asdic, in the hands of a trained operator, could determine the range and bearing of a submerged target. Importantly, however, it could not, at this stage, register its depth.

Ignoring the limitations of Asdic itself, but taking into account those of the U-boat, naval opinion, especially in Great Britain, greatly underestimated the threat that submarines again posed. This was encouraged further by Germany entering the war in 1939 with just 57 boats.

The primary anti-submarine (AS) weapon remained the depth charge, which had accounted for 30 U-boats during the earlier war. It was a simple drum, containing several hundred pounds of explosive and triggered by a hydrostatic switch at a predetermined depth.

This Asdic/depth charge combination had its own weaknesses. Fitted in a streamlined dome below a ship's forward keel, the Asdic transmitted pulses in a focused "beam", aimed downward at a fixed angle. For search purposes, it could be rotated in azimuth. Probing ahead at a fixed angle of declination, the Asdic inevitably lost contact some distance short of a submerged target. The attacker thus had to estimate the point, directly over the target, to release depth charges. Because the target's depth was not known, a "pattern" had to be dropped, set to explode at various depths. The charges themselves took time to sink and the cumulative "dead time" was sufficient to allow an astute submarine commander to manoeuvre clear of the lethal zone in good time, usually by a radical change of course.

What was required was a mortar-type weapon to project charges ahead of the ship, while the target was still "in the

ABOVE: Early depth charges were simple cylindrical containers that sank to the required depth painfully slowly. For any chance of success they were released in "patterns", being rolled over the stern from traps and fired on the beam from projectors. LEFT: An excellent example of the US Navy's graphic art, but note the "handraulic" loading and enlisted men apparently in dress suits. Reality in the Atlantic is more closely portrayed by the rig of the German ratings above.

beam". The need for this had been identified by British scientists between the wars but, due to budget restrictions, the concepts did not progress beyond the prototype stage. As a result, ahead-throwing weapons, in the shape of such as Hedgehog, Mousetrap and Parsnip, did not enter general service before the end of 1941.

Escort vessels to World War II

Between the wars, Great Britain was an enthusiastic supporter of naval limitation agreements even though many of the adopted clauses proved to be more detrimental to her own interests rather than to those of her peers and, increasingly, prospective enemies.

Following Jutland, the unrestricted German U-boat campaign had brought Britain to the brink of disaster before the timely institution (or, historically more correct, reinstitution) of the convoy system. The British failed, before the cessation of hostilities, to develop a viable detect-and-destroy means of countering the enemy submarines. Intense effort at the 1921–22 Washington Conference to dispose of the threat simply by banning submarine warfare was negated by late allies intent in preserving it as "the weapon of the weaker navy". In response, the British clung to the unsubstantiated belief that the introduction of Asdic (Sonar) on a general scale would remove the submarine as a major threat.

Even after the hard cull of destroyers following World War I, the Royal Navy still operated a total of 16 flotillas, or 144 ships. These were considered insufficient to both screen the battle fleet and to escort convoys, a situation made considerably worse by the London Naval Treaty of 1930, at which Britain and the United States agreed to capping global destroyer tonnage at 150,000 imperial tons apiece. Japan negotiated an improved 10:7 ratio for a total of 105,500 tons.

For the purpose of the Treaty, a "destroyer" was defined simply as having a standard displacement of less than 1,850 tons and mounting guns of under 130mm calibre. The agreed ceiling represented something like a further 25 per cent reduction in the Royal Navy's 16 flotilla establishment, exacerbating the convoy-escort situation.

ABOVE: **The German Navy continued to build both "destroyers" (for fleet work) and "torpedo boats" (effectively light destroyers) for general escort duties. Of the latter, four of the six Möwe class are seen pre-war with the two modernized Schlesiens behind.**

Fortunately, Article 8 of the Treaty stated that no limit would be placed on vessels of under 2,000 tons provided that, *inter alia,* they:
i) mounted no gun of greater than 155mm calibre;
ii) mounted no more than four of greater than 3in calibre;
iii) carried no apparatus for launching torpedoes; or
iv) were powered for no more than 20 knots' speed.

Within these stipulations are found the basic parameters of contemporary escorts ("sloops" in British parlance), particularly once (ii) was dropped at the largely ineffective Second London Naval Conference of 1936.

Britain, still in recession, required large numbers of inexpensive convoy escorts, and divided them between trawlers, dual-role mine-sweeping sloops, (e.g. Bangor, Halcyon and Algerine classes), true sloops (Grimsby, Bittern, Black Swan) and corvettes (Flowers), of which only the Bitterns and derivatives were governed by treat limits.

Largely locked in internal rivalry, the French and Italians pursued different roles, the former opting for fewer, but larger, destroyers and the latter more numerous escort destroyers. These, confusingly, were termed Torpedo Boats (*Torpediniere*). Fast and generally below 1,000 tons, they were well-suited to Mediterranean conditions.

Through the Anglo-German Naval Agreement of 1935, the Germans were legally permitted to build to 35 per cent of current British strength. In destroyers, that represented 52,000 tons. Disturbing though German rearmament was, this total, in conjunction with the rest of their naval programme, was unattainable. The Kriegsmarine likewise opted for a mix of fleet destroyers and "torpedo boats".

With war looking inevitable by 1938 the British Admiralty looked to expand the destroyer force, complementing the large and expensive six- and eight-gun fleet destroyers with smaller vessels designed specifically for escort duties. These "Intermediate Destroyers", the extensive Hunt class, were really the equivalent to foreign torpedo boats. Like the sloops, they mounted an effective high-angle armament but had a greatly superior speed and a modest torpedo battery.

The Americans had also been looking to produce an escort destroyer but, with the US Navy's inherent dislike for small ships (which in the words of the naval historian Norman Friedman "saved very little money at a great cost in capability") made little headway until the British requested 100 hulls in June 1941, effectively crash-starting the excellent Destroyer Escort (DE) programme.

TOP: **The Italian Navy rarely receives credit for its effective AS operations, 1940–43. These Spica-class torpedo boats (*Libra* and *Climene*) were typical of those which accounted for many Malta and Gibraltar-based British submarines.**
ABOVE: **Although launched in 1921, the Italian *Generale Achille Papa* could almost pass as a three-funnelled Royal Navy "L" boat of some seven years earlier. Constructed as destroyers, the Generali were demoted to torpedo boats in 1929.** BELOW: **An early example of a "Flower" with a long forecastle, HMS *Nasturtium* was one of three ordered from the design originators, Smiths Dock, to French account but purchased by the Admiralty in June 1940.**

ABOVE: **Classed as sloops by virtue of being relatively fast and being rated anti-aircraft escorts, the Black Swans proved to be most efficient anti-submarine ships. *Starling*, seen here, sank three U-boats and participated in the destruction of eleven others.**
RIGHT: **The British equivalent of foreign torpedo boats were the very useful Hunt classes (this is the Type I *Garth*). Their dual-purpose armament made them effective against aircraft.**

Atlantic experience – the emergence of the frigate

On the basis that slow-moving U-boats would waste too much time travelling to and from the deep ocean, it was assumed pre-war that they would concentrate around traffic nodal points fairly close to land. Convoy escort was, therefore, considered largely in coastal terms. Even so, restricted budgets had resulted in little being done before 1939 to develop prototypes suitable for emergency series production.

During that year an earlier proposal, to use a modified whaling ship, was reconsidered. Designed to operate independently in the Southern Ocean, these little ships were supremely seaworthy and, produced to commercial standards, were of a size that could be built by many small yards. These were not only in the United Kingdom but also in the less-developed marine industry of Canada.

In view of the looming inevitability of war as the 1930s progressed, it appears remarkable in retrospect that the orders for the first tranche of what were to become the Flowers were placed only in the late July of 1939.

In practice, Dönitz's U-boats did not operate entirely as expected, working ever further out into the Atlantic, not least to keep beyond the range of ASW aircraft. Intended for coastal escort, the Flowers thus found themselves in conditions to which they were not suited. Seaworthiness was not a problem for, although wet, a Corvette (as she became officially termed) could ride the worst of seas. In doing so, however, she had a

TOP: **By mid-1943, a high proportion of any Atlantic convoy would comprise standard, war-built ships. Laden with a low-density cargo and riding high, this unidentified Liberty ship was only one of over 2,700 built to the basic EC2-S-C1 specification.** ABOVE: **In addition to a huge Destroyer Escort (DE) programme, the Americans built about 100 Patrol Frigates (PFs) based on the British "River" design. *Anguilla* is one of 21 transferred to the Royal Navy, all of which were named after minor colonies.**

> "I was half-sitting and half-lying … my shoulders wedged … with the pitching of the ship, I seemed to be alternately reclining with my feet higher than my head, and then bending over so that I tended to fall forward." Alan Easton, shipper of the Canadian Flower-class corvette *Sackville*, from his autobiography *50 North*

motion that induced nausea and fatigue in crews already tolerating the spartan conditions inseparable from small ship life. Mess decks were rarely dry, often flooded.

The usual track from the British west coast to the Canadian convoy terminal of Halifax was 4,023km/2,500 miles. Routed evasively to avoid known U-boat concentrations, however, a convoy could cover nearer 4,828km/3,000 miles. A slow convoy could thus be 2½ weeks in transit, while the frequency of the convoy cycle saw several on passage simultaneously. Until more ships were forthcoming, the strain on an inadequate escort force was thus considerable.

Early Asdics (Sonars) were not of great range, perhaps 1.8km/1 mile in reasonable conditions and, as the periphery of even a small convoy was considerable, the two or three

ABOVE: **Where the 761/865-ton Type VIIC was Dönitz's general purpose, "workhorse" U-boat, the various larger Type IX were designed for lengthy patrols to say, the US eastern seaboard or the Caribbean. The ultimate IXC/40 displaced 1,144/1,257 tons.** RIGHT: **To those participating, convoys appeared to present enormous targets to enemy submarines. They were, however, mere specks in the immensity of the ocean and, with intelligence-based evasive routing, could be safely shepherded around known U-boat concentrations.**

LEFT: **Symbolically No.100, the American Destroyer Escort (DE) *Christopher* hits the Delaware River at Wilmington on June 19, 1943. Many DEs served with the Royal Navy, which considered them very satisfactory, but with a violent motion.** BELOW: **HMCS *Sackville*, preserved as a museum ship, is the sole surviving "Flower" and fittingly commemorates the enormous contribution in men and ships that Canada made toward ultimate victory in the bitterly contested Battle of the Atlantic.**

typically available escorts had to work hard to give effective cover. This meant working at speeds considerably greater than that of their charges, consuming extra fuel and diminishing endurance as a consequence.

To extend the escorts' range, Replenishment-At-Sea (RAS) was adopted. This in turn, however, exacerbated the problems of their over-crowded accommodation, the Flowers' designed complement of 29 having grown under operational conditions to no less than 74. The extended forecastle of the modified design improved matters in terms of both space and wetness, but the steady consumption of fuel oil and of topweight, represented by sixty 136kg/300lb depth charges, served only to increase a corvette's liveliness.

Because they could be built at so many yards (a total of 23 British and 12 Canadian yards was involved), Corvettes – Flowers, Modified Flowers and, later, Castles – were being completed right up to early 1945.

Despite their numbers, however, Corvettes had effectively been superseded from April 1942, with the entry into service of the first River. Of a size and speed with a Black Swan-class

sloop, this type was initially termed a Twin-screw Corvette before being reclassed as a Frigate (a title which, like Corvette, had been dormant since the days of the sailing navy). Still built to commercial standards, it was nearly half as long again as a Flower, with greatly reduced motion. Although the crew was larger, its amenities were much improved. To their considerable capacity of 150 depth charges was later added the forward-firing Hedgehog as it became available.

Operating on the surface, a U-boat could out-run a Flower, but not a 20-knot River, which also had better endurance. The simple but reliable 4-cylinder triple-expansion engine was, rather than the more complex turbine, selected for the great majority of both British- and Canadian-built escorts.

Convoy action – Battle of the Atlantic

Dönitz's tactics in the Atlantic included concentrating U-boats into groups or "Wolf Packs" which would form a patrol line across the anticipated track of a convoy. The boat making contact did not attack immediately but would vector-in the remainder to mount a simultaneous assault. Allied strategy, in turn, used intelligence to route convoys "evasively", around known U-boat concentrations. Although effective, this procedure did not always work.

On October 29, 1942, the 42-ship slow, east-bound SC 107 was nearing Cape Race, Newfoundland when it was seen and reported by *U-522*. The German radio intercept service had already discovered a mid-ocean rendezvous point for the convoy, and Dönitz now brought 14 boats together as Group *Veilchen* (Violet). These formed a line of search north-east of Newfoundland, awaiting the arrival of three further submarines.

On the 30th the local escort force handed responsibility for SC 107 to its ocean escort, the Canadian C-4 escort group. Even three years into the war, this comprised only one destroyer and four Flower-class corvettes, one of which was British. It was short of two units, one of which was the destroyer of the usual senior officer.

ABOVE: **The Royal Navy's "C" class of 1931 was curtailed at four ships. All were transferred to the Royal Canadian Navy, the *Comet* being renamed *Restigouche*. As an Atlantic escort, she has landed "Y" gun and her after tubes. Note the High Frequency Direction Finding (HF/DF) and Type 286 air search radar antennae.**

At this point, the convoy was still covered by land-based air and, working ahead, the Royal Canadian Air Force scored a notable opening success in exploiting German radio transmissions to surprise and sink the *Veilchen* boat *U-659* and the independent *U-520*.

Unfortunately, the short-range radio net used by the Allies to coordinate a convoy's defence was easily monitored by the attacking U-boats.

During the morning of November 1, SC 107 ran into the patrol line, whose *U-381* transmitted sighting reports. The escorts reacted immediately to make her submerge and to lose contact, but there were so many others in the area that, by dusk, five were in attacking positions.

German practice was to work on the surface by night, when their submarines' full speed could be utilized. The few early radar sets deployed by C-4 should have countered this, but all were unreliable or defective. Despite starshell illumination and determined intervention by individual escorts (two of whose COs had only five weeks' command experience), the enemy attacked boldly and continuously, torpedoing eight ships in 7 hours. Only one boat, *U-437*, was damaged sufficiently to oblige her retirement.

During November 2, the convoy was enveloped in thick fog and, despite being dogged by ten U-boats, lost only two further ships. A further Canadian corvette and a British destroyer arrived to buttress the escort.

LEFT: **Where a convoy might advance at only 8 knots or so, its escort, in rescuing survivors or investigating contacts, might fall well behind. A fast burst of speed to regain station could greatly deplete already limited bunkers.**

"Against such a scale of attack, a group of this kind cannot be expected to suffer other than heavy losses." Captain Hewlett Thebaud, US Navy, Senior Officer of US escorts based at Londonderry, commenting in writing on the report of SC 107's experience

Group *Veilchen* had not yet finished with SC 107. Attacking during the night of November 3/4, they took four more victims. One, an ammunition ship, exploded with such violence that it is believed to have destroyed her assailant, *U-132*, which disappeared without trace.

On November 4, the convoy's dedicated rescue vessel, loaded to capacity with over 300 survivors, was detached to Iceland with two escorts that were very low on fuel. One last ship was torpedoed and lost, but six U-boats had also to withdraw, themselves requiring fuel and torpedoes.

Finally having crossed the mid-Atlantic "air gap" on November 5, the convoy came under continuous air cover from Iceland, whence also arrived three American escort vessels. It proved to be the end of SC 107's travails, but the loss of 15 ships was serious and resulted in the British Admiralty, rather unfairly, severely criticizing the Canadians. SC 107's slow progress – it covered only 1,770km/1,100 miles in seven days, averaging 6 knots exposed it to a week of attack by up to 15 U-boats working together. C-4's ships were inadequate in numbers and, except for the destroyers, too slow. Their experience was limited and their defence was simply overwhelmed, just as Dönitz's tactics had intended.

The most effective procedure was to keep U-boats submerged, to prevent them using their relatively high surface speed and, thus, to lose contact. For this, more long-range maritime aircraft were urgently required.

RIGHT: **By October 1942 the battle against the U-boat was being won. Early aces such as Kretschmer (seen here), Schepke and Prien had been eliminated, and operational effectiveness was declining.**

ABOVE LEFT: **Designed as a heavy bomber, the B-24, or Consolidated Liberator, proved to be an outstanding success as a maritime patrol aircraft. Stripped to accommodate extra fuel, it could cover the notorious mid-Atlantic gap.** ABOVE: **From a small, peacetime nucleus, the Royal Canadian Navy expanded rapidly by its own effort to become a major force in the Western Atlantic. British and American criticism of its early shortcomings was, in retrospect, unduly harsh.** BELOW: **Dönitz's single-minded objective in targeting every possible merchant ship was, militarily, a brilliant strategy. A single ship might, for instance, be carrying more armoured vehicles than could be lost in a major tank battle.**

"Johnny" Walker and the Anti-submarine Support Group

In September 1941, Commander Frederick J. Walker was ordered to Liverpool to take command of HM sloop *Stork*, as a senior officer of the Western Approaches Command's 36th Escort Group.

Escort groups were a comparatively new concept, possible only with increasing numbers of escorts. Ideally homogeneous in terms of ship types, groups underwent brief but intensive training at Tobermory on Mull, Scotland, thereafter being kept together to develop a high degree of mutual understanding.

The primary duty of the senior officer of a convoy escort lay in the "safe and timely arrival" of his charges. With too few escorts, each stretched to its limit, the destruction of U-boats was secondary to just "keeping them down", where their low speed prevented their further intervention. Escort groups, however, comprised about eight ships (although, at any time, two might expect to be in dock) and the odd unit or two might usually be spared to prosecute a contact to conclusion. This was made clear in the Operational Instructions issued by Walker to his commanding officers. "The particular aim of the Group", he wrote, "is ... the destruction of any enemy which attacks the convoy." Walker's preferred methods involved several ships and a generous expenditure of depth charges.

It was already recognized that the presence of an Escort Carrier (CVE) acted as a force multiplier to enable an escort force to adequately cover the long perimeter of a convoy. The prototype British CVE, HMS *Audacity*, had already made her mark when, in December 1941, she was allocated, together with Walker's group, to the Gibraltar-UK convoy HG 76.

The 32-strong convoy passed beyond Gibraltar-based air cover on December 17, and, for four days, until it came within UK-based air cover, depended upon *Audacity*'s half-dozen fighters for local support. Besides forcing U-boats to submerge, the Martlets could also direct escorts to the spot. During four days of almost continuous action, Walker's ships were able to sink five U-boats. Although the carrier, a prime target, was lost, together with a destroyer and two merchantmen, it was a decided victory for the defence. In recognition, Walker was awarded the first of his eventual four Distinguished Service Orders.

LEFT: **During one of Walker's "rolling carpet" depth charge attacks, *Starling*'s after end could be a very busy place. The rapid replenishment of 136kg/300lb depth charges required dedicated team work, although conditions here are relatively benign.** ABOVE: **Stark though it was, Liverpool's Gladstone Dock was always a welcome sight to a weary Western Approaches escort. Admiral Sir Max Horton has "cleared lower decks" to cheer in the returning *Starling*. Her upper mast detail has been censored.**

LEFT: **Built to full naval, rather than mercantile, standards, the Black Swans and their improved successors were necessarily built in fewer numbers. Conspicuous on *Starling* is the aft-mounted "lantern" of her Type 271 surface-search radar.**
ABOVE: **No "gift horse" was ever better utilized. The first British escort carrier, *Audacity*, was remodelled from the captured German merchantman *Hannover*. Her career was short but she proved the value of a CVE in the defence of convoys.**

> **"No officer will ever be blamed by me for getting on with the job in hand." From Walker's Operational Instructions to the 36th Escort Group**

A series of convoy actions confirmed his methods and his determination but, already exhausted when promoted Captain in July 1942, Walker was rested in a shore billet for six months. Following his repeated requests for a further sea command, however, he was given the new sloop *Starling* in January 1943, transferring to her the experienced crew of the *Stork*.

With five others of her class, *Starling* formed the Second Support Group. Support groups differed from escort groups in being intended to reinforce the escort of any convoy that found itself strongly attacked.

Besides drilling his ships into a state of high efficiency, Walker developed new attack tactics. A problem with contemporary Asdic (Sonar) was that it lost contact for the final stage of an attack approach. Depth charges were thus dropped on an estimated position, with additional error being possible through "sinking time". Walker's method was to follow the target, at the same speed and at about 1,829km/2,000yd range. Aware of his Asdic, the submarine had no immediate reason to evade. One thousand yards ahead of Walker, however, steering the same course at a silent 5 knots, and

with Asdic secured, was a second sloop. Under Walker's direction, this vessel slowly overtook the unsuspecting target, rolling over a large depth charge pattern. Its detonation would be U-boat's first intimation of danger, usually too late to allow effective evasive action.

For deep-diving or "difficult" targets, a variation was to use three sloops in line abreast to release a lethal, rolling carpet of depth charges, saturating the whole target area.

Improved Sonars and ahead-throwing weapons largely cured the problem but Walker's ingenuity proved that it was possible to work effectively within the limitations of then-current equipment.

An inspirational leader, slated for flag rank but worn out by constant sea service, "Johnny" Walker collapsed and died in July 1944. He was just 48 years old.

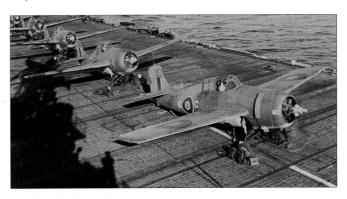

ABOVE: **Known to the US Navy as the Grumman F4F Wildcat, the Martlet entered service with the British Fleet Air Arm in 1940. Tough enough to withstand the rigours of carrier life, it served both with the fleet and, as here, on CVEs.**
LEFT: **The 2nd Escort Group seen from the *Starling*. *Loch Fada* is followed in order by *Wren*, *Dominica* and *Loch Killin*. The tall pole mast of the US-built *Dominica* contrasts with *Wren's* tripod and the *Loch's* sturdy lattice masts.**

Escort carrier Support Groups – taking the fight to the enemy

The first three years on the North Atlantic were all about survival, with inadequate and dangerously extended Allied AS resources covering UK-bound convoys in the face of unremitting submarine attack. This was Admiral Dönitz's chosen battleground, where his forces could destroy the greatest amount of tonnage for the least effort. Only reluctantly did he deploy extended-range boats farther afield, notably to the Caribbean and West Africa. In general, these forays resulted in fewer sinkings but were useful for their nuisance value, diverting scarce Allied defence resources.

With Allied war production getting into its stride, however, the North Atlantic and the Bay of Biscay transit area were, by mid-1943, becoming dangerous for U-boats. Dönitz responded by temporarily moving the centre of gravity of his operations southwards. Land-based aircraft from Bermuda, Morocco and Brazil proved inadequate (the Azores were not yet available) and the US Navy decided to allocate some of its earlier Escort Carriers (CVEs) to the theatre.

U-boats despatched to remote areas expended much time and fuel in transit and, to keep them on station longer, replenishment was required. It had been standard procedure for homeward-bound boats to transfer spare fuel or torpedoes to those remaining but the procedure was difficult. Special resupply submarines were thus built, notably the Type VIIF "torpedo carrier" and the Type XIV "U-tanker", which cruised the area, meeting depleted boats by appointment. They were

ABOVE: **During 1943 the US Navy formed five anti-submarine groups based on CVEs such as the *Block Island* (CVE-21). Known to the Americans as hunter-killer groups, they could operate independently by virtue of Ultra information.**

particularly valuable targets and, as their activities were frequently identified through Ultra signals intelligence, advantage was taken by the Allies now that the means had become available.

During the latter half of 1943 the US Navy created the first half-dozen "hunter-killer" groups, each based on an 18-knot CVE with about two dozen aircraft, usually Wildcats and Avengers. Four to six escorts were provided, latterly new Destroyer Escorts (DEs) but, initially, veteran "four pipers". Like the already constituted British Support Groups, the Americans were intended to reinforce dedicated convoy escorts when particularly threatened (notably on the US–Gibraltar route) but, otherwise, to seek out and destroy U-boats wherever they could be found. Before the advent of information from Ultra, such speculative hunts in a vast ocean were an impractical waste of resources but high-grade intelligence made specific targeting possible. Ultra, however, was neither guaranteed nor continuous, and the U-boats' greatest enemy continued to be the endless radio chatter generated by Dönitz's centralized control. All Allied AS vessels now sported the birdcage antenna of "Huff-Duff" (High Frequency Direction Finding, or HF/DF), which could give an accurate bearing on a transmitting boat.

LEFT: Successor to the F4F Wildcat, the F6F Hellcat became the US Navy's standard fighter from 1943. Working from CVEs, they strafed surface U-boats to suppress defensive fire while an Avenger approached with depth charges or homing torpedoes. BELOW: The Avenger torpedo-bomber built by Grumman was designated TBF or TBM depending upon its source of manufacture. Its cavernous ventral compartment could accommodate a full-sized 18in torpedo or 907kg/2,000lb of bombs.

> "Presence of escort aircraft carriers with the convoys make operating conditions so difficult for the U-boats that they are not likely to meet with success." Dönitz's Command War Diary, extract from entry for July 11, 1943

First on line was American Support Group 6, comprising the carrier *Bogue* and two veteran destroyers. They were joined at intervals by further groups based on the CVEs *Card*, *Core*, *Santee*, *Croatan* and *Block Island*. Their Wildcat fighters would typically surprise and strafe a surfaced U-boat to suppress return fire for a follow-up Avenger to deliver a knockout with depth charges or, increasingly, a "Fido" homing torpedo.

Allowed to roam freely within support distance of major convoy routes, the CVE groups achieved considerable success. Submarines were frequently caught on the surface in twos, or even threes, in the process of replenishment. It was far from being a turkey shoot, however, for many U-boats were now being armed with quadruple 2cm anti-aircraft guns and, in pressing home their attacks, many aircraft were heavily damaged or destroyed. Against the AS escorts, the Germans were also deploying acoustic torpedoes.

Remarkably, the only CVE lost on these profitable operations was the *Block Island*, destroyed by *U-549* with three conventional torpedoes. With a homing weapon, the latter then blasted the stern off an escort before herself succumbing to Hedgehog salvoes. The *Block Island* group had already accounted for six U-boats.

The CVE groups exploited the technical limitations and over-tight control of U-boats which, ultimately, were responsible for the failure of their campaign.

ABOVE LEFT: **A submariner of World War I, Admiral Dönitz ran a devastating U-boat campaign against the Allies. That it was ultimately adjudged fair was illustrated by Admiral Nimitz's testimonial on Dönitz's behalf during the post-war Nuremburg Tribunal.** ABOVE RIGHT: **Caught on the surface, a Type IX is lashed as she attempts to dive. Unfortunately for her, the aircraft would follow up with a depth charge salvo or a homing torpedo just ahead of the swirl that marked her submergence.** BELOW: **The sort of rendezvous that Support Group pilots dreamed of interrupting. In order to extend their patrols, operational U-boats were directed to meet up with Type XIV resupply boats for fuel, torpedoes and fresh stores.**

LEFT: **The 24 bombs of the Hedgehog were mounted on long spigots, angled so as to place the projectiles in a circular or elliptical pattern. As they exploded only on contact with a submerged target or the bottom, the bombs were not set for a specific depth.**

Improved weapons, sensors and escorts

As noted above, early Asdic (Sonar) had the unfortunate characteristic of losing contact with submerged targets at ranges below 100–150m/109–164yd. An AS vessel thus released depth charges on an estimated position, a shortcoming exacerbated by the time that the weapons took to sink to the desired depth. The result was "dead time", during which the target could take evasive action.

British Admiralty scientists were well aware of the Navy's problem, postulating that the solution lay in a mortar that could fire depth bombs ahead of a ship, while the target was still fixed in the Asdic beam.

During the 1930s a weapon was sea-tested and proved capable of throwing a small bomb up to a half-mile ahead. Although it was progressed no further, it led to proposals for two further weapons, a triple-barrelled mortar capable of firing three 200kg/440lb bombs, and a multi-way ejector throwing up to twenty smaller projectiles. From 1941 both concepts were given high priority.

The latter idea was the simpler, entering service late in 1941 as the Hedgehog. It fired 24 contact-fused bombs loaded on to spigots. Because of the powerful recoil forces, the bombs were electrically ripple-fired, the spigots aligned so as to drop them in a circle of some 35m/38yd diameter, centred

ABOVE: **Converted to a radar picket (DER), the American destroyer escort *Thomas J. Gary* retained her Hedgehog in the superfiring position forward. Further to a massive electronics upgrade, she has received an enclosed bridge and long amidships deckhouse.**

about 200m/218yd ahead of the ship. Each 30kg/65lb bomb contained half its weight of explosive, sufficient to hole a submarine hull. Somewhat more streamlined, the bomb sank twice as fast as a depth charge.

Hedgehog was initially very unpopular. Mounted on an exposed foredeck, it required constant maintenance. There was no reassuring "big bang" of a depth charge, unless the bombs actually contacted the target.

Hedgehog's first "kill", nonetheless, was in February 1942 and, by the end of the year, over 100 British ships had been so fitted. It was also adopted wholeheartedly by the US Navy.

"Anti-Dive Bombing Equipment."
Officially, the explanation to be given to casual enquirers of the purpose of Hedgehog during its secret introductory phase

---

By the end of the war, the kill rate for Hedgehog was six times that for conventional depth charges.

Improvements to U-boats included tougher hulls for deeper diving. There began to be doubts that the Hedgehog bomb was sufficiently lethal, and work was accelerated on the triple-barrelled mortar. Called Squid, this entered service in September 1943. Like that of the Hedgehog, the launcher was roll-stabilized, and its three bombs each weighed 180kg/390lb, again half of which was explosive. The projectiles fell in an equilateral triangle of side 35m/38yd, and centred some 250m/273yd ahead of the ship. They sank four times as rapidly as depth charges.

"Double Squid" proved to be particularly effective as, in plan, the two triangles formed a six-pointed star (i.e. with a relative offset of 60 degrees), with the two salvoes separated by about 20m/65ft in depth.

Squid was teamed with new Type 147 Asdic. This generated a precise, fan-shaped beam that could be depressed through a vertical range of 45 degrees. A specially adapted pen recorder gave a visual readout of range and depth of the contact. This data was communicated directly to Squid, which was fused and aligned automatically.

By the end of the war, Double Squid's kill rate was nudging 40 per cent. It was supplied to the US Navy, which service did not pursue it, preferring to rely on Hedgehog while it developed its own weapons.

A probable reason was that the system, with its magazines and handling spaces, was too demanding in space and weight to retrofit economically into large numbers of war-built ships. A major shortcoming was the tight design of the otherwise excellent destroyer escorts (DEs), making them unsuitable for modifications to accept Squid.

ABOVE LEFT: **The American Mousetrap was Hedgehog redesigned for smaller craft. The fierce recoil forces associated with firing the Hedgehog bombs was nullified by making the Mousetrap rounds rocket-propelled** TOP: **Designed around a double Squid installation, the British Lochs were given spacious accommodation for it forward of the bridge. *Loch More* was completed just before the war's end, but the class was greatly curtailed by cancellations.**
ABOVE: **Compared with that of a Loch (see above) the platform for a Castle-class single Squid was much shorter. "Castles" were too large to be built in Canada and were transferred from the Royal Navy. The Royal Canadian Navy's *Tillsonburg* was thus built as HMS *Pembroke Castle*.** BELOW: **The triple-barrelled Squid was built into a compact frame which allowed the weapon to be automatically roll-compensated. Barrels were angled to place the bombs in an equilateral triangle, and were lowered to the horizontal for loading.**

Fully committed to the weapon, the British designed the Loch-class frigate around the Double Squid and the Castle-class corvette around a single. Their firsts-of-class commissioned in December 1943 and September 1943 respectively. To accelerate the programme, Lochs were assembled from modules prefabricated in numerous facilities.

LEFT: **Type XXIs in the Blohm and Voss yard in Hamburg in May 1945. The fast electric boats, assembled from modules to production-line principles, posed a serious threat to the Allies but, fortunately, came too late to have any impact.**
ABOVE: **The head of an extensible Schnorkel for a Type XXI featured what was effectively a large ball-valve. The small stub on the top was to support a radar detector, and surfaces are meshed to reduce radar reflection and to improve flow.**

The emergence of the fast frigate

Early in 1943 the Germans acknowledged that convoy defences were getting the better of U-boats, and looked for a radical solution. The major shortcomings of existing boats were their very limited submerged endurance and speed, making it necessary to surface daily to recharge batteries, to renew the internal atmosphere, or to keep station on a convoy. Surfaced, and despite warning devices, they were vulnerable to detection and attack by increased numbers of aircraft, both shore-based and from escort carriers.

The resulting Type XXI U-boat was a major step forward in submarine design. Its large and deep hull contained three times the battery power of earlier boats while, externally, the hull was "cleaned-up" to minimize hydrodynamic drag. Schnorkel (or "Snort") was also under urgent development to permit extended submerged operation.

Tests predicted a Type XXI to be capable of submerged speeds of 18 knots for 1½ hours, or 12–14 knots for 10 hours. Hampered by surface conditions and the need to operate Asdic/Sonar, conventional convoy escorts would be unable to cope with such performance.

The Type XXI was assembled from large, prefabricated modules. These came from widely dispersed facilities and depended upon transport via inland waterways that were vulnerable to strategic bombing. This, together with acute shortages in skilled labour and materials, saw the production schedule slip to the point that the first-of-class "went operational" just four days before close of hostilities.

ABOVE: **Following the construction of two "hydrogen peroxide boats" to German principles, the Royal Navy abandoned the idea as impracticable. The ultimate goal would have been an atmosphere-independent boat, requiring no "Snort".**

Any relief at this, however, was short-lived for, with the immediate onset of the Cold War, the Soviet Union utilized captured German technology to produce a large submarine fleet of which the backbone were 236 Project 613, 644 and 665 known to NATO as the "W", or Whisky-class submarines and a near copy of the Type XXI.

Escalation to full hostilities would, once again, see Atlantic convoys as the keystone of Allied strategy, and a cash-strapped Royal Navy had to respond. The only new buildings that could be afforded were four each of Anti-Aircraft (AA) and Aircraft-Direction (AD) frigates. To provide fast frigates, capable

ABOVE: **A double Limbo installation in the after well of what appears to be a British Type 12 frigate. A major difference from Squid was that the weapons, fully stabilized in both roll and pitch, lifted their bombs over the ship's superstructure.** BELOW: **Converted to a Type 15 fast frigate, the British destroyer *Grenville* shows her Limbo installation. She was fitted with a small flight pad for initial experiments with a helicopter, in the interests of increasing stand-off capability.**

ABOVE: **The Type 81s (Tribals) were the first British frigates designed around a shipborne helicopter. The elevated flight pad, located well forward, formed the roof of deckhouse which became, via an elevator, the hangar for the aircraft.**

> "Sometimes, the exhaust clouds would turn from grey to black and then, to the stupefaction of all who saw them, suddenly erupt into cataclysmic fireballs of smoke and flame as the oxygen in the atmosphere completed the combustion begun inside *Explorer*."
> Report of surface trials with Britain's first hydrogen peroxide–fuelled submarine HMS *Explorer* (known to the Navy as *Exploder*!), quoted in *Daily Telegraph* of November 18, 1999

of meeting the new submarine threat, it was decided to convert some of the 32-knot war-built fleet destroyers, many of which had seen little service.

Suitably strengthened, these were capable of being driven at 25 knots in Atlantic conditions, while realizing a range of 5,311km/3,300 miles at 15 knots. The full conversion (Type 15) had an AS armament including Double Squid (or its successor, Limbo) and eight fixed tubes to launch the new Mark XX homing torpedo, which could work to the limit of range of contemporary sonars. Even these ships proved to be too expensive, so a limited conversion (Type 16) was produced in parallel. About two dozen destroyers were so modified between 1950 and 1958, but proved that speed alone did not provide the complete solution.

During the war, the Germans had persevered, but failed, in their attempts to produce a hydrogen peroxide-fuelled, turbine-driven submarine capable of bursts of very high submerged speed. The Soviets had also inherited this technology. All attempts to make it work failed ultimately, due to the dangerous instability of the fuel but, from 1954, emerged the even greater threat of the nuclear attack submarine (SSN). Somewhat slower than the abortive German hydrogen peroxide-fuelled "Walter" boat, the SSN had an effectively infinite submerged endurance and posed a far more serious problem.

As no affordable AS ship could realistically hope to track an SSN bent on evasion, the adopted solution was to build a slower frigate that deployed a rapid-reaction stand-off weapon. For a ship acting alone, the range of such equipment was limited to the useful range of the ship's sonar. The US Navy opted for a rocket-propelled missile (that became ASROC) which could compensate for long-range inaccuracy by its ability to carry a small nuclear warhead. The more radical British solution was to put a light helicopter aboard the ship. Since initial trials in 1956, frigate design has become ever more driven by helicopter requirements.

LEFT: **The superb all-round capability of large modern frigates, such as the German *Sachsen*, disguises their still-potent anti-submarine potential and tends to blur the distinction between destroyer and frigate as separate categories.** ABOVE: **An Australian-designed anti-submarine guided weapon, Ikara was purchased for the Royal Navy, with several Leander-class frigates being modified to deploy it. It works to maximum sonar range, releasing an American Mk 46 torpedo over the target's computed position.** BELOW: **Her duty done, the British Type 12 *Lowestoft* is expended as a submarine target. Anti-ship torpedoes are designed, not to hit a target, but to detonate under its keel. The shock of the explosion whips the ship in a longitudinal mode, breaking its back and causing structural failure.**

Frigates in the missile age

An obvious indication that, post-war, frigates were in a new age, was the virtual disappearance of superstructure in British designs. The thinking of the early Cold War included using nuclear warheads against groups of ships such as convoys or task groups. By the late 1950s, however, the need for useful topside space ensured that superstructures returned to something like normal.

With NATO standardization, frigates became Anti-Submarine (AS) specialists and destroyers Anti-Aircraft (AA). Both types, however, were expected to contribute to the firepower of a group while being able to defend themselves.

Heavy, tube-launched AS torpedoes soon lost favour, replaced by small, lightweight weapons which could be deployed effectively by shipboard helicopter as well as by tube. The helicopter became the ship's primary AS system, directed by the ship's hull-mounted and Variable Depth Sonars (VDSs).

As a less space-consuming alternative to the helicopter, the stand-off, shipboard AS missile looked attractive. The French, Soviet Union and United States developed their own, the British adopted the Australian Ikara. With ranges of 20km/ 12.5 miles or more, however, such weapons worked beyond the reliable range of the ship's sonar and the helicopter, instead of being made redundant, found a necessary alternative role in carrying a dipping (or "dunking") sonar to assist in targeting. There was then, of course, immediate pressure to increase the machine's size in order to carry weapons as well, a complex data link, and a crew of two to work it all. For a submarine hunt, two helicopters are infinitely

more effective, while conferring a measure of redundancy. The effect on frigate size was dramatic.

The introduction of the gas turbine as a main propulsion unit in the 1960s was a revolution. Its great advantages include its ability to start from cold in a matter of minutes, its compactness and relatively light weight. It suffers from a higher initial cost and its narrow efficiency bands, necessitating separate main and cruising turbines. Repair is by replacement, much reducing time spent in dockyard hands. An extra bonus is the reduction in engine room personnel, representing a considerable saving in through-life costs as well as in accommodation space.

LEFT: **The impact of a shipborne helicopter on a frigate's design is enormous, fully 30 per cent of the *Iron Duke*'s length being devoted to the upkeep and operation of her Merlin helicopter. Fully loaded, the aircraft weighs 14.3 tons, compared with a Lynx's 4.6 tons.** ABOVE: **The current American Littoral Combat Ship project will result in an unconventional multi-purpose, high-speed vessel with interchangeable weapons systems. The General Dynamics *Independence* trimaran is shown here, one of three contenders.**

Frigates continue to provide designers with a dilemma. Ideally, a design is compact and inexpensive, necessary for series production in an emergency. In reality, however, all modern systems are demanding in volume, driving up size and cost. The more valuable the ship, the greater the case for comprehensive "defensive armament", so space is made for up to eight canister-launched anti-ship missiles. Earlier attempts to save space by eliminating the sole remaining dual-purpose gun came to nought when, in 1982, the Falklands War was a reminder of just how indispensable it was, and remains.

Anti-ship missiles are getting ever more sophisticated and, currently, considerable effort is being devoted to "stealth" measures to reduce frigates' radar signatures. While this produces some striking designs it is possible that the effectiveness of the measures will be outweighed by their inhibiting effects on a ship's utility.

Bearing in mind that the helicopter remains the frigate's primary AS weapons and targeting platform, it makes sense to configure the ship to facilitate the operability of the aircraft across the greatest range of sea states. Since the inception of the shipborne helicopter, however, it has been the practice, almost without exception, to locate the helicopter right aft, where it is subject to the maximum accelerations and amplitude of movement. Experimental trimaran ship forms promise a steadier platform with considerable amidships deck space, hulls of reduced resistance and significantly reduced heat signatures.

ABOVE: **One of the 46-ship Knox class of frigate, the USS *Aylwin* (FF-1081) is seen launching an ASROC missile. The 8-cell Mk.116 launcher was modified to launch Harpoon SSMs in addition, but has been superseded by Vertical Launching System (VLS).** BELOW: **The acutely raked stem of the Russian *Neustrashimy* indicates a sizeable, low-frequency bow sonar. The hump right aft, abaft the flight pad, covers the winch and stowage for a variable-depth sonar and passive towed array. As with German frigates, freeboard is generous.**

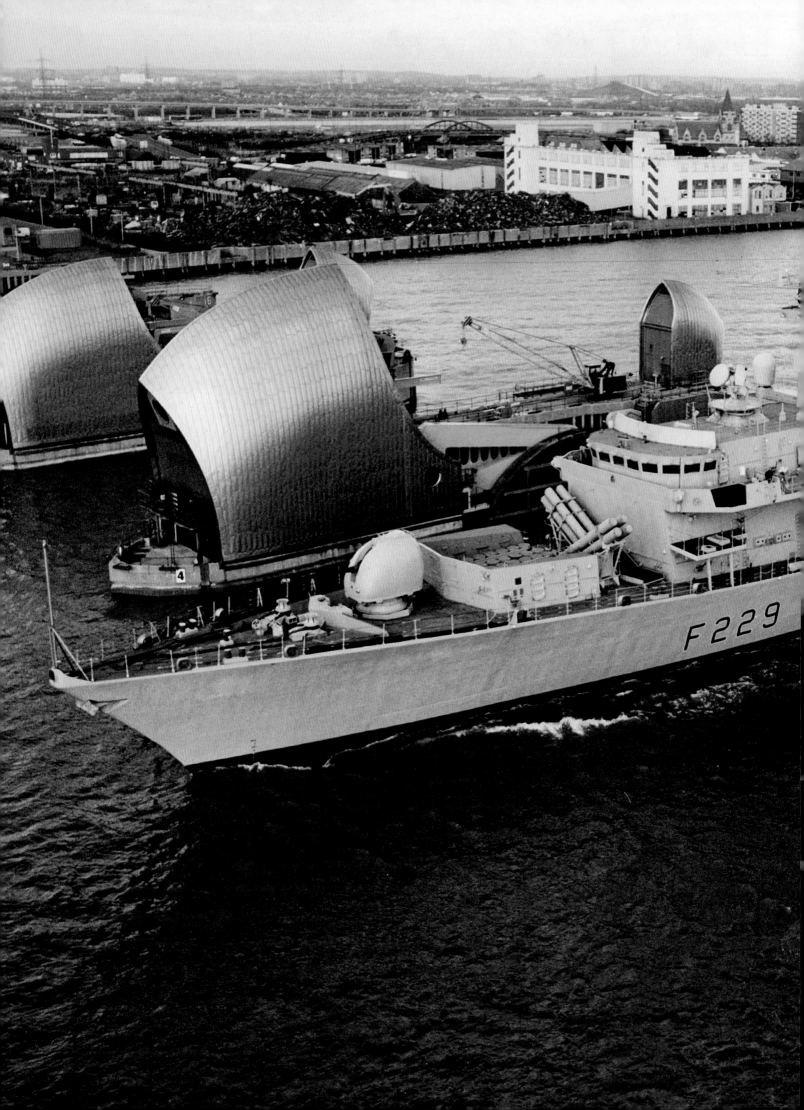

A Directory of Frigates

For the purposes of this book, the term "frigate" is synonymous with "escort", including as it does the various sloops, corvettes, torpedo boats/escort destroyers/destroyer escorts that were concerned primarily with the safe passage of commerce and, by extension, taking the war to the submarines bent on its destruction. Space, regrettably, forbids the inclusion of the considerable classes of ocean minesweeper and "Admiralty trawler" which, although performing admirably as escorts, cannot be considered frigates.

The eventual employment of convoy during World War I resulted in the development of the first dedicated escorts, uncomplicated ships designed for humdrum routine, releasing destroyers to the business for which they were better suited. The Battle of the Atlantic underlined the need for "large corvettes", combining range and capacity with seaworthiness, simplicity and cheapness. Thus emerged the frigate, a further feature of which was its suitability to be series-built in large numbers.

With the formation of NATO, all primarily Anti-Submarine (AS) escorts became generically termed "frigates", in contradistinction to "destroyers", which were now configured primarily around Anti-Aircraft Warfare (AAW).

LEFT: **HMS *Lancaster*, a Type 23 frigate, passes the Thames flood barrier on a port visit to London. As a general-purpose frigate, her AS capacity resides in her helicopter and shipboard torpedo tubes. Note the Harpoon and Sea Wolf VLS forward.**

LEFT: **In a distinctive Western Approaches camouflage scheme, *Crane* is seen here "swinging compasses". The censor has deleted the HF/DF antenna at the masthead, the communications antenna at the yardarm extremities and the pendant number.** BELOW: **Badly shot-up during the "Yangtze Incident", *Amethyst* was repaired in time to participate in the Korean War. Bridge personnel and gun crews, clad in anti-flash gear, stand by in anticipation of yet another bombardment detail.**

Black Swan and Modified Black Swan classes

Fine ships, the Black Swan sloops tended to be built by destroyer yards. They were designed for the AA protection of convoys, for which they carried the very effective twin 4in high-angle (HA) Mk X1X mounting, four in the earliest examples, three in the remainder, with a quadruple 2pdr pompom in lieu of "Y" guns. Together with full director control, this amounted to a considerable aggregation of topweight and this, with the requirement for a slow, easy roll (to make a good gun platform) gave designers a challenging stability problem. Active fin stabilizers, not yet very effective, were fitted but hostilities saw a creeping increase in complement and topweight, necessitating an extra 30cm/1ft of beam in the "modified" subclass, with the omission of splinter protection and some boats.

Extra weight included a proliferation of light, automatic weapons and a lattice mainmast bearing the "lantern" of the Type 271/272 surface warning radar. Depth charge capacity also increased, from 40 with two projectors in early units to 110 and eight respectively.

The design did not readily lend itself to later modification for a forward-firing Squid mortar, taking instead a split Hedgehog, located either side of "B" mounting. Despite this, the Black Swans were deadly submarine hunters. Based mainly at Liverpool and Greenock, they were fully or partly responsible for 28 kills, many by Captain "Johnny" Walker's redoubtable 2nd Escort Group. Afterdeck arrangements were cramped by the Admiralty requirement that a proportion of the class should be capable of minesweeping.

Steam-turbine propelled, they had good acceleration and were handy in manoeuvring. At "convoy" speeds, they had an endurance of about 13,800km/7,500nm.

Thirteen original and twenty-four modified Black Swans were built, six to Indian account. Five were cancelled and, although hard-worked, only four were lost.

LEFT: **Seen shortly after World War II, the Modified Black Swan *Peacock* enters Grand Harbour, Malta. She retains her old-style "U" flag superior and the original depth charge arrangements. Split Hedgehog was carried forward but the class did not get Squid.**

Modified Black Swan class, as designed

Displacement: 1,350 tons (standard); 1,960 tons (full load)
Length: 86.3m/283ft (bp); 91.3m/299ft 6in (oa)
Beam: 11.7m/38ft 6in
Draught: 3.5m/11ft 4in
Armament: 6 x 4in guns (3x2), 4/6 x 40mm guns (2x2/2x1)
Machinery: Geared steam turbines, 2 boilers, 2 shafts
Power: 3,208kW/4,300shp for 19.5 knots
Endurance: 420 tons for 11,220km/6,100nm at 15 knots
Protection: Nominal
Complement: 210

Hunt classes

The Black Swans were officially termed Convoy Escorts; the Hunts, Fast Escorts. Where the sloops traded speed for capacity, the Fast Escorts were small destroyers, smaller but considerably faster than the sloops, carrying the same powerful AA battery but lacking their great endurance. They were intended to undertake all destroyer activities short of fleet work.

Over-worked constructive staff unfortunately made a fundamental error in stability calculation. On being inclined, the first-of-class was obliged to land "X" gun mounting, shorten the funnel and to reduce the upper structure. These measures, together with 50 tons of permanent ballast, were sufficient, and 22 of these Type I Hunts were built.

The Type Is were seen as deficient in armament, however, so that follow-on Type IIs were made a considerable 76cm/30in beamier. This cost about three knots in speed, but allowed the reinstatement of the third mounting and an improved bridge layout. This programme ran to 34 units.

As the war obliged Hunts to undertake duties for which they were not intended, torpedo tubes were demanded. This resulted in the 28 Type IIIs, with a twin 21in torpedo tube mounting, but reverting to only two twin 4in mountings, in "A" and "X" positions. Funnel and masts were set vertically, without rake.

The two Type IVs were not related, being Thornycroft "specials", Nearly 5m/16ft 5in longer, and beamier, they

ABOVE: **Steaming past an interned Italian battleship in Malta, the *Tanatside* shows the characteristics of the Type III Hunts, vertical funnel and mast, "Y" gun mounting suppressed, but with a twin torpedo tube mounting added amidships.**

could carry the full specified six-gun AA battery and three of the desired four torpedo tubes. With similar machinery, however, they were slower. Their major innovation was to continue the forecastle deck three-quarters aft, making for a stronger and more comfortable (if hotter) ship. The pronounced forward knuckle was not successful.

The Hunts performed very effectively, particularly in support of English East Coast and Mediterranean convoys. Nearly one in four was lost.

ABOVE: **The Type I Hunts, typified by *Meynell*, came out badly overweight. Torpedo tubes and "X" 4in gun mounting were sacrificed, funnel shortened and director lowered. Although employed on the East Coast, she has the Type 271 radar lantern and the "Huff-Duff" aerial of an ocean escort.**

Type II Hunt class, as built

Displacement: 1,050 tons (standard); 1,420 tons (full load)
Length: 80.6m/264ft 3in (bp); 85.4m/280ft (oa)
Beam: 9.6m/31ft 6in
Draught: 3.4m/11ft (mean)
Armament: 6 x 4in guns (3x2); 1 x quadruple 2pdr pompom
Machinery: Geared steam turbines, 2 boilers, 2 shafts
Power: 14,174kW/19,000shp for 25.5 knots
Endurance: 277 tons fuel for 4,630km/2,500nm at 20 knots
Protection: Nominal
Complement: 164

LEFT: **Still looking very "mercantile", the 1941-built *Jasmine* has been given a long forecastle but still has the original flimsy bridge structure and mast ahead of it. Engaged in convoy escort, she has her whaler griped but turned out for instant use.**

Flower class

Although immortalized by their role in the Battle of the Atlantic, the Flowers were intended to be coastal escorts. Built largely to mercantile, rather than Admiralty standards, their hull was based on a stretched version of a Smiths Dock whale catcher. Their size and class meant that they could be built by many yards, British and Canadian, with no previous experience of warship construction. Already in production, they were involved in ocean warfare in the absence of anything more suitable.

Expected also to double as minesweepers, early examples had a short forecastle, with a single bandstand-mounted 4in gun. The after sheer was pronounced; the forward, less so. Like trawlers, they had a deeper after draught to give the hull "bite" and the single, large-diameter propeller adequate immersion. Propulsion was by a simple steam reciprocating engine, but lacking both redundancy and size, a Flower could not expect to survive torpedo damage.

There was a distinctly mercantile air about early Flowers, with their cowl ventilators, flimsy glazed wood wheelhouse and foremast ahead of it. Later ships were improved with much longer forecastles, modified forward sections and an "Admiralty" bridge.

They were amazingly seaworthy little ships but had a rapid and pronounced movement that fatigued the best of crews. Living conditions, already spartan, were frequently made worse by flooding.

Flowers were built in yards ranging from the mighty Harland & Wolff to tiny slips up obscure Canadian creeks.

ABOVE: ***Vetch***, as shown in 1942, has gained a more "naval" bridge structure, radar and a relocated mast. She carries her escort group number on her funnel. The 2pdr gun has a good all-round arc of fire.

With little shipbuilding tradition, the contribution of Canada to the Atlantic battle is worthy of great credit, their 121 (many improved) Flowers being just one element. The many British yards involved constructed a further 145. Most were completed by 1942, with construction moving on to frigates and the improved Castle-class corvette. Flowers are credited with sinking 53 enemy submarines; 35 became war losses.

LEFT: **HMCS *Oakville* is a reminder of the great contribution made by the Canadians to victory in the Battle of the Atlantic. In total, 121 Flowers stemmed from Canadian yards. Note the American-sourced anchor.**

Flower class, with long forecastles

Displacement: 1,015 tons (standard); 1,220 tons (full load)
Length: 58.9m/193ft (bp); 63.5m/208ft 4in (oa)
Beam: 10.1m/33ft 1in
Draught: 4.2m/13ft 9in (mean)
Armament: 1 x 4in gun; 1 x Hedgehog AS spigot mortar (later)
Machinery: 1 x 4-cylinder triple-expansion steam engine, 2 boilers, 1 shaft
Power: 2,052kW/2,750ihp for 16 knots
Endurance: 230 tons oil for 6,480km/3,500nm at 12 knots
Protection: None
Complement: 85

River class

Even as the Flowers first demonstrated their limitations under ocean conditions, a more appropriate type was under development. To pursue a surfaced submarine, or to quickly regain station, an escort really required 22 knots rather than the Flowers' 16. As this would require steam turbine propulsion, however, it was decided to compromise with a "twin-screw corvette", capable of 20 knots with a Flower-type reciprocating engine on each shaft. Only in 1942 was their extra speed and capability recognized by recoining the historic term "frigate".

Even 20 knots demanded an increase of nearly 50 per cent in hull length, so that many of the small, corvette builders could not construct the new ships, all named after British rivers. This was

remedied, however, by the United States building the design as its Patrol Frigate (PF). Of these, 21 were transferred to the Royal Navy as the Colony class.

Dimensioned around full minesweeping gear, the Rivers' spacious afterdeck was able to accommodate over 200 depth charges. A full Hedgehog was carried forward, but very exposed. Later fitting of a double Squid was intended, but eventually applied to just one ship.

Larger escorts such as frigates were also expected to contribute to the AA defence of a convoy. To the single 4in low-angle guns of the surface armament was thus added an eclectic range of automatic weapons. The mix depended upon availability but only latterly included 40mm Bofors to replace pompoms and Oerlikons.

In addition to the universal "Huff-Duff" direction-finding antenna, all sported the Type 271 "lantern", later superseded by the tilting "dish" antenna of the improved Type 277.

In all, there were 57 British-built Rivers, 45 Canadian and 22 Australian. There were 77 American PFs. Five Rivers were lost, but accounted for 18 submarines.

RIGHT: *Antigonish* **was one of 70 Rivers built in Canada. Following post-war modification, she has been built up aft to create a well for Squid, has a twin 4in gun forward and an enclosed bridge, more appropriate to Canadian weather conditions.**

River class, as designed

Displacement: 1,400 tons (standard); 1,925 tons (full load)
Length: 86.3m/283ft (bp); 91.9m/301ft 4in (oa)
Beam: 11.1m/36ft 6in
Draught: 3.9m/12ft 10in (mean)
Armament: 2 x 4in guns (2x1/1x2); 1 x Hedgehog AS mortar
Machinery: 2 x 4-cylinder triple-expansion steam reciprocating engines, 2 boilers, 2 shafts
Power: 4,103kW/5,500ihp for 20 knots
Endurance: 646 tons for 13,335km/7,200nm at 12 knots
Protection: Nominal
Complement: 114

LEFT: **In a late World War II paint scheme,** *Leeds Castle* **shows her clear Flower ancestry. With a full frigate-type bridge structure and long, easy sheer, there is little "mercantile" left except, perhaps, the cowl ventilators over the machinery space.** ABOVE: **It is 1946, but** *Bamborough Castle* **still looks weather-worn and carries her wartime-style pendant number. The robust lattice mast still supports a Type 272, where** *Leeds Castle* **(left) has a later Type 277, its dish laid horizontally.**

Castle class

Designed to rectify the shortcomings of the Flowers, the Castles were some 15m/50ft longer, placing them halfway between a Flower and a River. Still to be built by many small, unsophisticated yards, they were designed for construction by traditional methods, rather than by the pre-fabrication then becoming general.

Dating from late 1942, the Castle design was able to incorporate features proven by early Rivers. The forward end had a sweeping flare and sheer, with the forecastle deck continued well aft. The quarterdeck, made more spacious by an adaptation of the Rivers' triangular transom, was enclosed by a solid bulwark. There was a full naval bridge structure, and an amidships lattice mast supporting the Type 272 (later 277) radar antenna at an effective height. Visually, the Castles were very attractive.

The class was designed around the new Squid mortar, the *Hadleigh Castle* being the first to take it to sea operationally, in August 1943. Only a single Squid could be accommodated, located in the elevated "B" position and superfiring an improved single 4in gun. Because of the (fully justified) confidence placed in Squid, the depth charge arrangements were much reduced.

Unseen, the Castles accommodated their major advantage, the Type 147Q Asdic (Sonar) that could continuously feed the Squid system with range, bearing and depth, "holding" a submerged target up to the mount of firing three, fast-sinking bombs.

For simplicity of production, the propulsion unit was the same type of reciprocating engine that powered both the Flowers and Rivers, though with improved, water-tube boilers.

Maturing rather late in the war, the Castle programme was drastically curtailed, only 39 being completed as corvettes. Fifteen from British yards were cancelled, as were all thirty-six ordered from Canadian yards. Twelve British-built Castles were transferred to Canada, and one to the Norwegian flag.

ABOVE: *Hadleigh Castle* **as a new ship in late 1943. The single Squid, on the platform forward of the bridge, is not obvious. Although few depth charges needed to be carried, she had a wide, uncluttered afterdeck.**

Castle class	
Displacement: 1,080 tons (standard); 1,580 tons (full load)	
Length: 68.6m/225ft (bp); 76.9m/252ft (oa)	
Beam: 11.1m/36ft 6in	
Draught: 4.1m/13ft 6in (mean)	
Armament: 1 x 4in gun; 1 x 3-barrelled Squid AS mortar	
Machinery: 1 x 4-cylinder triple-expansion, steam-reciprocating engine, 2 boilers, 1 shaft	
Power: 2,051kW/2,750ihp for 16.5 knots	
Endurance: 480 tons oil for 11,480km/6,200nm at 15 knots	
Protection: Nominal	
Complement: 100	

ABOVE LEFT: **This picture of *Loch Killisport* shows that only a single 4in gun is carried, located on a bandstand. There is no director, but a quadruple 2pdr pompom is sited aft.** ABOVE: **For philatelic artwork, this rendering of *St. Austell Bay* is surprisingly accurate. It indicates well the crank level with the bridge at the commencement of the straight line sheer. Lapped plates are, however, shown where the hull was, in fact, all-welded.** LEFT: **The Bays were AA variants of the Lochs. As can be seen here on *Mounts Bay*, the double Squid was suppressed in favour of a Hedgehog in "A" position. Two twin 4in guns are carried, together with full director control and Type 293 radar.**

Loch and Bay classes

The Rivers confirmed the optimum size for a North Atlantic escort, but there continued to exist the urgent need for numbers. These could be produced only by redesigning for construction from prefabricated modules, fitted out to rigidly standard specification. The resulting Loch-class frigates thus comprised large numbers of elements, none heavier than 3 tons, produced by non-shipbuilding concerns and transported to dedicated assembly and fitting-out facilities. Complex curvature was avoided, the result retaining River-class characteristics but with greater sheer and flare forward.

Larger, of course, than a Castle (to which there was a distinct resemblance),

a Loch could accommodate a double Squid in the elevated "B" position. The associated Asdic, which made the system so deadly, was situated adjacently, in an office extending from the bridge front. As the depth charge outfit was, again, much reduced, it left adequate space aft for the first crude countermeasures ("Foxers"), designed to meet the threat of the acoustic torpedoes with which U-boats were now targeting convoy escorts specifically.

Only one 4in gun was carried, on a bandstand where it could be depressed easily to engage very close-range targets. The after centreline position was occupied by a quadruple 2pdr pompom with an excellent field of fire.

By the time that the first-of-class, *Loch Fada*, was completed at the end of 1943, the conventional U-boat was a spent force. Only 31 hulls were, therefore, completed as Lochs but, despite their limited numbers, they still accounted for 16 of the enemy.

With emphasis shifting to Pacific operations, the next 19 hulls were completed as Bay-class AA escorts, with Squids suppressed in favour of a Hedgehog, but with a twin 4in mounting at either end and two sided twin 40mm Bofors. These proved their worth during the Korean War, which involved considerable bombardment details.

Loch class, as built	

Displacement: 1,430 tons (standard); 2,260 tons (full load)
Length: 87.2m/286ft (bp); 93.7m/307ft 4in (oa)
Beam: 11.7m/38ft 6in
Draught: 3.8m/12ft 4in (mean)
Armament: 1 x 4in gun; 1 x quadruple 2pdr pompom; 2 x 3-barrelled Squid AS mortars
Machinery: 2 x 4-cylinder triple-expansion, steam-reciprocating engines, 2 boilers, 2 shafts
Power: 4,103kW/5,500ihp for 19.5 knots
Endurance: 725 tons oil for 12,965km/7,000nm at 15 knots
Protection: Nominal
Complement: 114

ABOVE: **Six surplus Lochs were acquired by the Royal New Zealand Navy in 1948. Here, a pristine *Rotoiti* retains her original Royal Navy pendant number as *Loch Katrine*. Post-war, all frigates took an "F" flag superior.**

Types 15 and 16

Although the German fast submarine programme was delayed sufficiently for it to have little effect on World War II, the Soviet Union's acquisition and exploitation of the associated technology posed a new threat, the more real with the outbreak of the Korean War. Faced again with the prospect of general war, the Royal Navy needed a new generation of escort, fast enough to deal with high-speed submarines. Funds, however, were sufficient only for the conversion of war-built fleet destroyers to "fast AS frigates".

Full conversions, eventually numbering 23, were known as Type 15s, the programme running from 1949 to 1956. Remodelling was very thorough, the selected hulls being razed to upper-deck level. To tolerate the requirement of being driven into a head sea at 25 knots, the bow section was stiffened and the forecastle extended to over 80 per cent aft. At its after end were two staggered pockets housing Squid AS mortars, later replaced by Limbos.

The Bikini A-bomb trials had highlighted the effect of nuclear blast, so superstructure was restricted to just one level above the forecastle deck. All needed to be enclosed, causing bridge personnel difficulties in navigation.

Cleared of all except anchor gear, foredecks were given two breakwaters and a curved bridge front. Armament was reduced to a twin 4in mounting aft and a twin 40mm Bofors atop the bridge. Ships were fitted for, rarely with, up to eight sided tubes for homing torpedoes. Much of the new topside structure was

ABOVE: **AS high-speed convoy escorts, the Type 15s were designed to co-operate with aircraft in countering the fast submarine.** *Wakeful* **here, has the full standard outfit. Note how the line of the original destroyer hull can be clearly discerned.**
LEFT: **An ice-dusted** *Virago* **is seen in the Arctic during the 1950s. The conditions point to the weakness of having the wheelhouse set so low. A double Squid and twin 4in guns were located aft, with only a twin 40mm gun forward.**

in aluminium alloy. The original machinery and funnel were retained.

Less thoroughly rebuilt were the ten Type 16s. These had higher, frigate-style bridges and a twin 4in in "B" position. Their forecastles were not extended, the original forward set of tubes being retained for AS torpedoes. Two Squids were located aft.

U-class destroyer, as Type 15 AS frigate

Displacement: 2,200 tons (standard); 2,700 tons (full load)
Length: 103.5m/339ft 6in (bp); 110.6m/362ft 9in (oa)
Beam: 10.9m/35ft 9in
Draught: 4.9m/16ft
Armament: 2 x 4in guns (1x2); 2 x 3-barrelled Limbo AS mortars; 8 x heavyweight (8x1) or 6 x lightweight (2x3) AS torpedo tubes
Machinery: Geared steam turbines, 2 boilers, 2 shafts
Power: 29,840kW/40,000shp for 36.5 knots
Endurance: 585 tons for 5,370km/2,900nm at 20 knots
Protection: Nominal
Complement: 185

ABOVE: **The Type 16 limited conversions were just that. The ships retained their destroyer-like characteristics being able, as this picture of** *Termagent* **shows, even to remount their torpedo tubes. Gun armament has, however, been drastically reduced, the after deckhouse accommodating a Double Squid.**

LEFT: **Termed "Second Rate" frigates to differentiate them from such as the big Type 12s, the Type 14s (or Blackwoods)** were really an updated and (relatively) cheap corvette. Despite single screw and rudder, *Hardy* shows her manoeuvring qualities. ABOVE: **The Type 14s were often criticized for being under-armed and, as this picture of *Duncan* shows, there was little to see beyond the two Limbo mortars. Disposal of a damaged, surfaced submarine would have been a problem.**

Type 14

Budgets boosted by the threat posed by the Korean War, the Royal Navy embarked on a relatively ambitious frigate building programme during the 1950s. To the "de luxe", but stop-gap, Type 15/16s needed to be added a simple convoy AS escort, capable of being produced in quantity in emergency. Earlier, the Type 14 or Blackwood, would have been called a "corvette"; in new terminology, it was classed a Second-Rate Frigate.

Designed to a cost limit, the Type 14 was the smallest that could accommodate a double Limbo and full sonar outfit, while being large and fast enough to deploy them effectively against a 17-knot (submerged) submarine. The result looked, and was, utilitarian.

A raised forecastle extended 50 per cent of her length, topped by a full-width house upon which was set the diminutive bridge. This arrangement resulted in a two-level transition to the bridge deck, which made the after end appear to lack freeboard. A single, vertical funnel served to two boilers of the half-frigate propulsion plant. For compactness, diesel engines were considered, but rejected on cost grounds. There was a single shaft and rudder.

The two Limbos, which occupied the after end, were protected by bulwarks and deckhouse, but wetness was such that an overhead catwalk connected after superstructure and forecastle, while a solid bulwark was provided right forward. Anchors were recessed.

Controversially, the Type 14s did not carry a medium-calibre gun. Submarines forced to the surface would thus need to be finished by torpedo, for which paired tubes, unusually of large calibre, were sided in the waist.

Although only 12 of a planned 23 were built, they were deemed successful although, by today's standards, service aboard was spartan. Fine-lined and fast, if somewhat fragile, they made their mark in fishery protection.

LEFT: **In the late 1960s, *Exmouth* was converted into a trials ship for gas turbine propulsion. One sprint Olympus and two cruise Proteus were installed COGOG fashion. Note how the ducting dominated the topsides of so small a ship.**

Type 14, as designed

Displacement: 1,100 tons (standard); 1,460 tons (full load)
Length: 91.5m/300ft (bp); 94.6m/310ft (oa)
Beam: 10.1m/33ft
Draught: 3.1m/10ft
Armament: 3 x 40mm guns (3x1); 2 x 3-barrelled Limbo AS mortars; 4 x 21in AS torpedo tubes (2x2)
Machinery: Geared steam turbines, 2 boilers, 1 shaft
Power: 11,190kW/15,000shp for 24.5 knots
Endurance: 260 tons oil for 8,335km/4,500nm at 12 knots
Protection: None
Complement: 111

LEFT: **Types 41 and 61 shared a common hull, being fitted out either for anti-aircraft (Type 41) or aircraft-direction duties. Designed for convoy duties, both were diesel-propelled.** *Salisbury*, **a Type 61, shows her comprehensive electronics fit.**

Types 41 and 61

Even with the end of hostilities in 1945, the defence of trade, specifically convoys, still loomed large with the Admiralty Board. The dual-function Loch/Bay programme had impressed, producing numerous hulls quickly and relatively cheaply. They had, however, already been rendered obsolete by the arrival of the fast submarine and jet aircraft. ASW would need to be addressed by faster ships, but the Board also required a hull that could be fitted out for AAW or for the control of carrier-borne or shore-based aircraft. As both of these functions were aimed primarily at the defence of convoys, a 25-knot maximum speed would suffice, with emphasis being placed instead on endurance and good seakeeping.

Endurance was conferred with diesel propulsion. Three machinery spaces accommodated no less than ten engines, four of which could be coupled to each of two shafts. The remaining pair powered generators.

A high-freeboard hull took the forecastle deck right aft to a point just forward of a short quarterdeck. Forward of the break was a pocket containing a single Squid. The chosen medium-calibre weapon was the new Mk VI twin 4.5in gun. The size and weight of this mounting resulted in the unusually cranked forward sheerline. This gave the required freeboard while lowering the weight of the gunhouse in relation to the hull for stability purposes. It also allowed the personnel in the new-style, low-level bridge to see over it. There were no conventional funnels, the diesel exhausts led up the inside of the lattice masts.

Only four of each type were built for the Royal Navy. The AAW version (Type 41/Leopard class) was roll-stabilized with two twin 4.5in guns. The AD (Aircraft-Direction Type 61/Salisbury class) had half the firepower but an impressive array of electronics, later extensively modernized.

LEFT: **This is the Type 41** *Puma*, **as completed, with a second twin 4.5in gunhouse aft. The mainmast was later plated-in to support a single 965 radar. Note the "two ball" daymark to indicate that she is engaged in towage.**

Type 41

Displacement: 2,225 tons (standard); 2,525 tons (full load)
Length: 100.7m/330ft (wl); 103.7m/339ft 11in (oa)
Beam: 12.2m/40ft
Draught: 3.3m/10ft 10in (mean)
Armament: 4 x 4.5in guns (2x2); 1 x 3-barrelled Squid AS mortar
Machinery: 8 diesel engines, 2 shafts
Power: 11,190kW/15,000bhp for 23 knots
Endurance: 230 tons fuel for 8,335km/4,500nm at 15 knots
Protection: Nominal
Complement: 221

INSET RIGHT: **Built as essentially general-purpose frigates, the Leanders were also given major conversions for specialization in either surface or AS warfare. Here,** *Penelope* **of the former group shows Exocets and a shrouded Sea Wolf launcher.** RIGHT: **The basic Leander design, an Improved Type 12, sold well for export. Here, the Royal New Zealand Navy's** *Wellington* **prepares to refuel from the replenishment tanker** *Endeavour*. **Note her sister** *Canterbury* **in the background.**

Type 12/Leander class

To run alongside the Types 41/61 frigates, a new ASW ship was required, fast enough to counter the expected Soviet HTP (High Test Peroxide) closed-cycle submarines. The best compromise was the 28-knot Type 12, essentially a similar hull form, but with an extended and fine-sectioned bow. Steam-driven with a standardized and compact machinery outfit, these required a conventional funnel, initially thin and vertical, later, and less successfully, larger.

Excellent Sonar was teamed with two Limbos, located in a deep pocket where the long forecastle terminated, well aft. Sided in the waist were, initially, no less than 12 heavyweight AS torpedo tubes

but, with the failure of the weapon itself, these were replaced by tripled small-calibre tubes, not always carried.

From 1966 the Wasp helicopter became the delivery platform for highspeed, stand-off reaction to submerged contacts. The Type 12's forward Limbo was landed and part of the well decked-over to provide a flight deck. The after superstructure was converted to a hangar and topped with the four-rail Sea Cat point-defence SAM, a not-too successful replacement for the 40mm Bofors.

The Improved Type 12, or Leander, class used the same hull form (later units were given 61cm/2ft more beam) and machinery. Full freeboard extended right

aft, but with a transom notch for VDS. A solid, compact superstructure had plated-in masts, the mainmast supporting a "single bedstead" of the Type 965 air warning radar. A small helicopter, Sea Cat and a single Limbo were incorporated from the outset.

Of the twenty-six Leanders built for the Royal Navy, eight were later converted to deploy the Australian Ikara stand-off AS missile. Seven more were remodelled around the MM38 Exocet SSM, with a further five taking both Exocet and the Sea Wolf point-defence SAM.

Magnificent seaboats, the Leanders also sold well abroad.

ABOVE: **An early Type 12,** *Scarborough*, **with the original small funnel. To minimize the effects of nuclear blast, the upperworks were deliberately made very low. The long, high-freeboard bow design made them magnificent seaboats. She is seen at Malta with an American Coontz-class DDG.**

Leander class, as designed

Displacement: 2,305 tons (standard); 2,875 tons (full load)
Length: 109.8m/360ft (wl); 112.9m/370ft (oa)
Beam: 12.5m/41ft
Draught: 4.1m/13ft 4in (mean)
Armament: 2 x 4.5in guns (1x2); 2 x Sea Cat 4-rail SAM launchers; 6 x 325mm AS torpedo tubes (2x3)
Machinery: Geared steam turbines, 2 boilers, 2 shafts
Power: 22,380kW/30,000shp for 28 knots
Endurance: 480 tons oil for 8,335km/4,500nm at 12 knots
Protection: Nominal
Complement: 258

Type 21

The Admiralty's own resources being at full stretch, Vosper-Thornycroft's gas turbine Mark 5 frigates, built for Iran, were made the starting point for the new Type 21, intended as a replacement for the aging Types 41 and 61 and, possibly as a follow-on to the Leanders. The Admiralty Board was convinced that it could thus acquire a cheaper, but equally capable, ship. It couldn't, but the reduced complement resulting from gas-turbine propulsion certainly effected a real through-life saving.

Two Olympus engines were supplied for sprint speeds, and two Tynes for cruising. Even derated, the former delivered power for an unusually high speed of 30 knots. The forward end, otherwise conventional, was thus given

a pronounced knuckle to throw water clear, while the anchors were set high and in pockets.

Rakish rather than handsome, the Type 21s had a full-width superstructure deck which dropped to a broad-transomed afterdeck, giving relatively generous space for a small helicopter. Much of the superstructure was of load-bearing aluminium alloy which, in service, proved liable to fatigue cracking, weakening the hull girder.

Forward was a single 4.5in gun of the new fully automatic Mk VIII design. Superfiring it, on most of the eight ships, were four MM38 Exocet SSM launchers. On the hangar roof was a quadruple Sea Cat SAM launcher. The primary ASW system was the Lynx helicopter, capable

ABOVE: **Safeguarding vital tanker traffic during the Iran–Iraq War was but one of the Royal Navy's duties, discharged here by *Active*. The controversial industry-designed Type 21s were the first British all-gas turbine frigates.**

of carrying a limited combination of weapons, sensors and datalink. It was supported by its ship's sonar and two sets of AS torpedo tubes.

A single, plated-in mast was located amidships and the after superstructure was dominated by the single large funnel and its associated downtakes. Accommodations were spacious, adding to the ships' popularity.

The design proved to have little margin for updating, and all six survivors were sold to Pakistan in 1993–94.

LEFT: **The class lead ship, *Amazon*, replenishes at sea. Four Exocets superfire the forward 4.5in gun, and the Sea Cat mounting is visible aft. All structure above upper deck level was of aluminium alloy, the hull requiring subsequent stiffening.**

Type 21, as designed

Displacement: 2,750 tons (standard); 3,250 tons (full load)

Length: 109.8m/360ft (wl); 117.1m/384ft (oa)

Beam: 12.7m/41ft 8in

Draught: 5.9m/19ft 6in (maximum)

Armament: 1 x 4.5in gun; 4 x Exocet MM38 SSMs (4x1); 1 x quadruple Sea Cat SAM; 6 x 325mm AS torpedo tubes (2x3)

Machinery: 2 Olympus and 2 Tyne gas turbines, 2 shafts

Power: 37,300kW/50,000shp for 30 knots

Endurance: 7,410km/4,000nm at 17 knots

Protection: Nominal

Complement: 175

LEFT: **One of the Batch I Type 22s, *Brazen*'s dimensions were limited by home dockyard covered facilities. Designed as successors to the Leanders, they were gas-turbine driven and carried fewer crew members, but were considerably larger.** BELOW: **Built as a replacement for Falklands War losses, *London* was a Batch II ship whose major differences, besides upgraded electronics, were a remodelled bow section to accommodate improved sonar, and facilities for a larger helicopter. Note the lack of a gun.**

Type 22

Originally as Anglo-Dutch project, from which the Dutch withdrew, the Type 22 was intended as close escort for high-value vessels. The hull was designed around the two 45.8x3.1m/150x10ft arrays of the Type 2016 sonar, one of which was located on either side of the keel. The primary AS weapons delivery system was the helicopter (one/two Lynx or one Sea King), backed by shipboard AS torpedo tubes.

At either end was a Sea Wolf point-defence SAM system, capable of engaging incoming missiles as well as aircraft. There was no space for a medium-calibre gun but four MM38 Exocets were located forward.

Two Olympus and two Tyne gas turbines were again arranged COGOG fashion, exhausting through a single funnel of considerable dimensions.

Only four of these "Batch I" units were built before it was decided to significantly upgrade capability by adding both towed array and new (Type 2015) bow-mounted Sonars. The former required a widened transom, enabling helicopter facilities to be extended, possibly for the future Merlin. The bow Sonar dictated a heavily raked bow profile and stem anchor.

Electronic Counter and Support Measures (ECM/ESM) were also greatly improved. The machinery fit was changed to a more economic pair of Spey gas turbines for sprint with two Tynes retained for cruising. Termed "Batch IIs", six were built.

Following the loss of two Type 42s and two Type 21s during the Falklands War, four further Type 22s were built as replacements. These, known as

"Batch IIIs", added a 4.5in gun (found indispensable in the shore support role) and Harpoon SSMs in place of Exocets. These were relocated amidships.

Only the Batch IIIs remain in the Royal Navy. The four Batch Is were sold to Brazil and two Batch IIs each to Chile and Romania. One has been scrapped and one expended as a target.

ABOVE: **Sharing a common hull form with the Batch IIs, the Batch III *Cornwall* has been given a 4.5in gun. Exocets have been replaced by Harpoon, relocated abaft the bridge and thus releasing valuable space on the foredeck. The carrier is the American CVN.74 *John C. Stennis*.**

Type 22, Batch III

Displacement: 4,280 tons (standard); 4,850 tons (full load)

Length: 135.7m/445ft 4in (bp); 148.1m/486ft 2in (oa)

Beam: 14.8m/48ft 5in

Draught: 6.4m/21ft (max)

Armament: 1 x 4.5in gun; 8 x Harpoon SSM (2x4); 2 x sextuple Sea Wolf SAM; 1 x 30mm Goalkeeper CIWS; 6 x 325mm AS torpedo tubes (2x3)

Machinery: 2 Spey and 2 Tyne gas turbines (COGOG), 2 shafts

Power: 35,957kW/48,200shp for 30 knots.

Endurance: 700 tons fuel for 12,965km/7,000nm at 18 knots

Protection: Nominal

Complement: 232

Type 23

The Type 23 began as an austere vessel, designed around the major task of deploying a passive towed array sonar for sustained periods. Such has been the pace of the Royal Navy's retrenchment, however, that the design grew into a full-specification frigate, necessarily filling the gap left by Leander disposals. Size and cost escalation nonetheless demanded that, where there were 26 Leanders, there were but 16 Type 23s. These were launched over a 13-year period, with early units being sold abroad just five years after the last ones hit the water.

The remainder are capable, multi-purpose frigates whose subtle, signature-reducing features have resulted in an appearance both pleasing and business-like. Their major combat system is the Merlin ASW helicopter, whose size demands a generously dimensioned flight pad, from beneath which the towed array is streamed. Anti-submarine torpedo tubes are carried, as is an active, bow-mounted sonar.

The single 4.5in dual-purpose gun forward is backed by eight Harpoon SSMs, sited forward of the bridge. Between is the Vertical-Launch System (VLS) containing 32 Sea Wolf point-defence SAMs, whose all-round control is exercised by directors both forward and aft. Two 30mm cannon flank the structure forward of the large, angular funnel, which is wider than it is long.

Two Spey gas turbines drive generators to provide the power for the electric propulsion motors built around the shafts. Emergency, get-you-home power may also be diverted from the ships' four diesel generators. Because the electric propulsion units may be reversed, variable-pitch propellers are not necessary, their fixed-pitch alternatives being optimized to run most quietly over the ships' most sensitive speed range. The final ten of the class have a 25 per cent greater propulsion power, increasing speed by possibly 2 knots. Every effort has been made to minimize crew strength.

ABOVE: **Type 23s have a much-reduced radar signature, even to giving the hull a flare over its full length.** *Lancaster* **has the well-tried Mk VIII 4.5in gun, but all will receive the new Mod. 1 version with the "radar-reduced" angular shield. These will be issued to all units as they come to major refit.**

Final ten of Type 23 class

Displacement: 3,600 tons (standard); 4,300 tons (full load)
Length: 123m/403ft 9in (bp); 133m/436ft 7in (oa)
Beam: 15m/49ft 3in
Draught: 5.5m/18ft 1in (maximum)
Armament: 1 x 4.5in gun; 8 x Harpoon SSM (2x4); 1 x 32-cell Sea Wolf SAM VLS; 6 x 325mm AS torpedo tubes (2x3)
Machinery: 2 Spey gas turbine/generators driving electric propulsion motors, 2 shafts
Power: 39,015kW/52,300shp for 30 knots
Endurance: 800 tons fuel for 14,445km/7,800nm at 17 knots
Protection: Nominal
Complement: 185

LEFT: **During the course of their careers, the E50s and E52s underwent so many modifications that they became difficult to differentiate.** *Le Corse,* **here, shows the E50s' early "trademark" of four triple AS torpedo tubes forward.**

Le Corse and Le Normand classes

Much of a size with the British-sourced River-class frigates that they superseded, these were the first significant post-war classes built by the French with funding supplied partially by the Americans under their Mutual Defence Assistance Programme.

The four le Corse (E50) types and the 14 le Normands (E52) had a common hull and machinery fit, differing only in their armament disposition. Both types were classified "fast escorts" and carried both AA and AS outfits of considerable potency for the size of ship.

Their hulls were flush-decked, with pronounced forward sheer, a form possibly influenced by the ex-American Destroyer Escorts (DEs) which were also

still serving under French colours. In line with the then-current assumptions on the likelihood of nuclear exchanges, neither the monolithic bridge structure nor the hulls were pierced for scuttles.

Besides a quadruple or sextuple mortar (two in the E50s) the major AS weapons resided in four triple torpedo tube mountings. In the E50s, these were all forward of the bridge at 01 level, backing on to structures containing reloads. The E52s carried theirs in a more orthodox arrangement, sided in the waist. This created space for a forward-mounted mortar.

Both classes carried three twin 57mm dual-purpose gun mountings, one forward and two in superfiring

arrangement aft. Steam turbine propulsion gave a good turn of speed, and the taller, prominently capped funnel located close to the mast differentiated them immediately from Commandant Rivière-class frigates with which they could be confused.

During 20 years of service, individual units began to differ widely in detail, *le Brestois* for instance acting as trials ship for the single 100mm gun that went on to be widely adopted in French warships, and *l'Agenais* trialling a large VDS installation in lieu of the after guns.

By 1981, none of either class remained on the active list.

ABOVE: *Le Picard* was an E52, this photograph showing clearly that the four triple AS torpedo tubes are located in more protected positions, sided in the after waist. Note the sextuple AS launcher forward. The 57mm armament was effective only against aircraft.

E52 type, as built

Displacement: 1,295 tons (standard); 1,795 tons (full load)
Length: 95m/311ft 10in (bp); 99.3m/325ft 11in (oa)
Beam: 10.3m/33ft 10in
Draught: 4.1m/13ft 6in (maximum)
Armament: 6 x 57mm guns (3x2);
    1 x 4- or 6-barrelled 305mm AS mortar;
    12 x AS torpedo tubes (4x3)
Machinery: Geared steam turbines,
    2 boilers, 2 shafts
Power: 14,920kW/20,000shp for 28.5 knots
Endurance: 310 tons oil for 8,335km/4,500nm
    at 12 knots
Protection: Nominal
Complement: 175

FAR LEFT: **The *Commandant Rivière* class followed the E52s quickly and, while only slightly larger, differed considerably. The dual-purpose 100mm guns were effective against aircraft and surface craft, while diesel propulsion conferred greater range.** ABOVE: **During the early 1970s, the *Balny* acted as the trials ship for gas turbine propulsion. Although echoing *Exmouth*'s role in the Royal Navy, she had a gas turbine and diesel (COGAD) arrangement as opposed to the British ship's COGOG.**

Commandant Rivière class

Specialist in series small-ship production, Lorient naval dockyard, which had built eight of the E50/52s, went on to construct all nine of the Commandant Rivière-type follow-ons.

The later ships were to act in peace time as "avisos", station ships in the still-numerous French colonies. In this sense, they were the lineal descendants of the colonial cruisers, the sailing corvettes of a different era.

For the sake of required speed, the E50/52s were relatively fine, while their pronounced forward sheer would have translated somewhat uncomfortably to the accommodation deck below. The Rivières' hull was made about 4m/13ft 2in longer but proportionately more beamy. Unlike that of the preceding class, the deckhouse extended to the ships' sides, the foredock accommodating a 100mm gun. The extra space was required to transport and support up to 80 troops, for whom two small Landing Craft, Personnel (LCP) could be carried under davits.

Essential to colonial duty was extended endurance and reliability. For this reason, they were powered by four medium-speed diesel engines. These were coupled two to a shaft, making it possible to run with any combination of one to four units. Any could thus be taken off-line for routine maintenance while, together, they could power the ships for 25.5 knots, sufficient for them to act as useful escorts in wartime.

The *Commandant Bory* and *Balny* performed the same role as the *Exmouth* of the Royal Navy in being trials platforms for gas turbine propulsion. Work concluded, they were refitted with standard diesel units.

As built, the Rivières had three of the new 100mm guns, in single, automatic, enclosed mountings, in place of the earlier ships' twin 57mm mountings. From the late 1970s most exchanged "X" gun for four MM38 Exocet SSMs. An enclosed quadruple AS mortar occupied "B" position. The class was scrapped during 1988–92.

MIDDLE: ***Doudart de Lagrée* at her full 25-knot speed. Note the "X" gun replaced by four Exocets, the French-built quadruple AS mortar and reload facility in "B" position, and the triple AS torpedo tubes sided abaft the funnel.** ABOVE: **Oblique lighting picks out the effects of years of stress on the hull of *Enseigne de Vaisseau Henry*. The large full-width deckhouse allows the carriage of an 80-man marine unit or, in their absence, spacious accommodation, welcome on what frequently acted as station ships.**

Commandant Rivière class, as designed

Displacement: 1,750 tons (standard); 2,250 tons (full load)
Length: 98m/321ft 8in (bp); 103.7m/340ft 4in (oa)
Beam: 11.6m/38ft 1in
Draught: 4.6m/15ft 2in (maximum)
Armament: 3 x 100mm guns (3x1); 1 x 4-barrelled 305mm AS mortar; 6 x AS torpedo tubes (2x3)
Machinery: 4 diesel engines, 2 shafts
Power: 11,936kW/16,000bhp for 25.5 knots
Endurance: 210 tons for 13,890km/7,500nm at 16 knots
Protection: Nominal
Complement: 166

LEFT: **A one-off, the Aconit was very unusual for a ship of her size in having single-shaft propulsion. In this early picture she mounts an AS projector forward of the bridge and Malafon (not visible) amidships.**

Aconit

Her original status indicated by her name, one of the British-built Flower-class corvettes manned by Free French crews, the *Aconit* nonetheless carried full frigate capability, indicated by an "F" identifier. Despite her single shaft and anti-submarine configuration, however, she looked more like a destroyer, and soon adopted a "D" flag superior. Her task was, primarily, to act as a trials platform for the larger Tourville-class destroyers then building.

Aconit's hull was flush-decked, dropping one level to a short afterdeck, whereon was accommodated the large winch/towfish assembly of the DUBV 43 Variable Depth Sonar (VDS). The bows showed the pronounced overhang associated with a large bow sonar, also

incorporating the flattened sheerline that enabled the forward gun to work at slight depression for close ranges.

She was the first to be designed around the Malafon AS stand-off system, following its satisfactory trials in the converted destroyer *La Galissonnière*. Destined for the new Tourville and Suffren classes, Malafon was a small, rocket-propelled, aerodynamic vehicle that could release a homing torpedo on coordinates determined by the ship's sonars.

For self-defence, *Aconit* had launchers for AS torpedoes and, forward of the bridge, an enclosed quadruple AS mortar. The latter was removed during the early 1980s in favour of eight updated MM40 Exocet SSMs, grouped in two quadruple protective boxes.

Although lacking an AA missile system, the *Aconit* was dominated by the large tower and dome associated with the DRBV 13 (later DRBV 15) surveillance radar, and the antenna of the DRBV 22A targeting radar on the lattice mast on the after superstructure.

Being steam propelled, *Aconit* had a conventional funnel although, in order to conserve centreline deck space, this had to support a lofty, and complex foremast, an ungainly arrangement.

Along with the Malafon system itself, the *Aconit* was retired in the mid-1990s, her name being quickly reassigned to a La Fayette-class frigate, perpetuating a unique Anglo-French naval link.

LEFT: **With modernization during 1984–85, the Aconit had eight MM40 Exocets fitted, visible here inside protective boxes. Malafon remained as there was no helicopter, but a new VDS and passive towed array were installed aft.**

Aconit, as built

Displacement: 3,500 tons (standard); 3,840 tons (full load)
Length: 127m/416ft 10in (oa)
Beam: 13.4m/44ft
Draught: 5.5m/18ft 1in (maximum)
Armament: 2 x 100mm guns (2x1); 1 x Malafon AS stand-off system; 1 x quadruple 305mm AS mortar; 2 x launchers for AS torpedoes
Machinery: Geared steam turbines, 2 boilers, 1 shaft
Power: 21,373kW/28,650shp for 27 knots
Endurance: 9,260km/5,000nm at 18 knots
Protection: Nominal
Complement: 255

D'Estienne d'Orves class

Although twin-screwed and carrying "F" pendants, the d'Estienne d'Orves, or A69, class are strictly corvettes, designed for inshore AS operations. They began to commission in 1976 as the first E50/52s reached about 21 years of age and, thereafter, replaced them on a near one-for-one basis. Considerably smaller, however, they are also less capable, their design being strongly driven by the requirement for economical operation. Through-life costs have been reduced considerably by their diesel propulsion and a crew of only 100. Classed as "avisos", their lack of size has, nevertheless, been a drawback in that their additional full 18-man military detachment apparently cannot, in practice, be supported.

Compact little ships, their single 100mm gun looks disproportionately large. The low bridge structure is integral with a long, full-width deckhouse. Not having space for a helicopter, their AS capability is, by current standards, weak.

Four fixed AS torpedo tubes are built into the after superstructure, but the quadruple AS mortar on top has now been removed in favour of light AA missiles, either the capable Crotale or the much lighter, two-rail Simbad. Only one, hull-mounted sonar is fitted.

Originally termed A70s, some units were fitted with two MM38 Exocets. This variant disappeared as all were gradually fitted for, but not always with, two of the later MM40s which would, however, require a third party in order to realize their full over-the-horizon potential. This greater emphasis on light escort ("frégate légère") function is underlined by the addition of defensive anti-missile and anti-torpedo decoy systems.

TOP: **An early picture of *d'Estienne d'Orves*, lead ship of an excellent class of twin-screw corvette. The 100mm gun was standard throughout the French Navy and was a useful yardstick in estimating a ship's size.** ABOVE: **Unusually carrying no pendant number, the nameship here looks more weatherworn and retains her short funnel. Note the caps of the AS torpedo tubes in the after deckhouse, atop which is a sextuple Bofors-pattern AS rocket launcher.**

Ordered originally by South Africa, two more units were purchased by Argentina, which then built a third. Seven have now been retired and one transferred to Turkey. All of the remainder are due to be paid off by 2016.

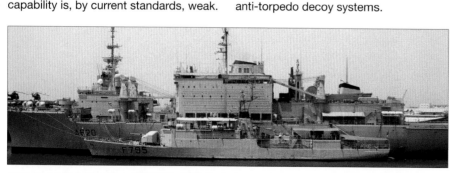

ABOVE: **During Operation "Desert Shield" in 1990, the *Commandant Ducuing* is seen with the later raised funnel and mast. She lays alongside repair ship *Jules Verne*, with a Durance AOR beyond (right) and Clemenceau carrier (left). In Gulf conditions, large-ship facilities are welcome to small-ship crews.**

A69, as built

Displacement: 1,050 tons (standard); 1,250 tons (full load)
Length: 76m/249ft 6in (bp); 80m/262ft 7in (oa)
Beam: 10.3m/33ft 10in
Draught: 5.3m/17ft 4in (maximum)
Armament: 1 x 100mm gun; 1 x quadruple/ sextuple AS mortar; 4 x fixed AS torpedo tubes
Machinery: 2 diesel engines, 2 shafts
Power: 8,335kW/12,000bhp for 23 knots
Endurance: 8,280km/4,500nm at 15 knots
Protection: Nominal
Complement: 100

LEFT: **Larger and more comfortable for lengthy seatime than the d'Estienne d'Orves type, the Floréal-class corvettes are designed more as offshore patrol vessels. The Moroccan *Mohammed V* was one of two built to a reduced export specification.** ABOVE: **Here, the Moroccan *Mohammed V* is led by her sister the *Hassan II*. In armament and electronics, they have a lower capability than the French Floréals but are similar otherwise. Note the 76mm guns and rather dated WM-25 fire control.**

Floréal class

With ever-fewer front-line warships available, their use can no longer be justified for low-risk duties such as fishery protection or colonial policing. Rather limited as "avisos", the A69s were more useful as escorts in the Mediterranean. The Floréals, which effectively replaced them in patrolling the overseas territories, were built more cheaply to mercantile standards, constructed at St. Nazaire but fitted with their military equipment in the Lorient naval dockyard. Named after months of the New Revolutionary Calendar, all were commissioned in 1992–94.

In length, the Floréals are pitched between the A69s and the E50/52s that preceded them in colonial duties. Being designed for only 20 knots, however, they are relatively beamy (L/B 6.09 compared with the 23-knot A69's 7.38 and the 26-knot E50's 8.31), with a capacious hull. This allows the A69's major shortcomings to be addressed. Up to 24 military personnel may be carried, along with an LCP under davits. Where smaller, utility helicopters are usually deployed, the hangar has the capacity to accommodate either an AS.332 Super Puma transport helicopter or, if required, an NH-90 AS machine. The ships are not fitted with sonar or AS weapons but can carry two MM38 Exocets and a Simbad/Mistral SAM system.

The aircraft hangar runs forward between the sided uptakes which have mercantile-style tops. The hull is flush-decked, a form much disguised by the long, full-width "centre-castle". This terminates short of the stern, suggesting that, in emergency, the ships could be fitted with a large towed array passive Sonar for surveillance purposes. Forward, the rather limited freeboard is compensated by a pronounced flare. Active stabilizers reduce ship motion.

All six carry a single 100mm automatic gun with optronic fire control. They are fitted to ship two MM38 Exocets and/or one Simbad/Mistral point-defence SAM mounting.

ABOVE: **"Regular" Floréals carry a 100mm gun, more modern electronics and are fitted for, but not necessarily with, two Exocet SSMs. Their considerable internal space results in a bulky hull that gives the effect of low-freeboard bows. This is *Prairial*, the "month of meadows" and ninth in the New Calendar.**

Floréal class, as built

Displacement: 2,600 tons (standard); 2,950 tons (full load)
Length: 85.2m/279ft 8in (bp); 93.5m/306ft 11in (oa)
Beam: 14m/45ft 11in
Draught: 4.4m/14ft 5in
Armament: 1 x 100mm gun; 2 x MM38 Exocet SSM; 1 x twin-rail Simbad SAM
Machinery: 4 diesel engines, 2 shafts
Power: 6,565kW/8,800shp for 20 knots
Endurance: 390 tons fuel for 18,520km/10,000nm at 15 knots
Protection: Nominal
Complement: 83

LEFT: **Lead ship of the class, *la Fayette* has lowered shutters covering the mooring ports forward. The boat aperture may also be screened. A pair of Exocets are visible amidships and, to their left, the launcher for the Crotale point-defence SAM.**
ABOVE: **The latest of many French warships to bear the name *Surcouf* is seen in the Gulf in 2002, serving as part of a multinational force. Note how the hull and upperworks are not pierced with scuttles, and also the newly profiled 100mm gunhouse.**

La Fayette class

Although much of a size with a British Type 42, a la Fayette appears somewhat smaller by virtue of her radically different appearance and lack of detail. There had been a growing trend toward inclining surfaces in order to reduce radar return, particularly to defeat the active homing radar of anti-ship missiles. The la Fayettes took the concept a stage further, with an outer shell configured to screen all the many minor protuberances that, collectively, define a ship's radar signature. Their hulls have a continuous flare and the extensive inclined planes of the superstructure are fabricated from a radar-absorbent sandwich. All apertures, such as those for access, for boat stowage, anchor pockets, etc are covered by flush-fitting doors as tightly engineered as those of an automobile, and likely as vulnerable to contact damage.

Diesel propulsion has again been specified, considerably simplifying problems associated with hot exhaust emissions while improving both economy and endurance. The cost, however, is a mediocre maximum speed.

Like the smaller Floréals, the la Fayettes normally carry no AS sensors or armament. They can accommodate a 25-strong military detachment and are fitted for colonial duties. Current peacetime armament comprises a 100mm gun forward (its enclosure reconfigured to further reduce reflection), two quadruple MM40 Exocet SSM launchers (behind deep bulwarks amidships) and an 8-cell Crotale point-defence SAM mounting on the hangar roof. A Panther multi-purpose helicopter is normally carried, but facilities are adequate to accommodate the larger NH-90 AS helicopter if required for specific tasking.

The half deck between gun and bridge front marks a covered cavity into which can be slotted a double 8-cell VLS for the smaller type of ASTER SAMs, probably not normally fitted.

Six modified and more heavily armed versions were built for Taiwan (1994–96) and three for Saudi Arabia (2000–02).

ABOVE: **Model-like in her simplicity of form, the *la Fayette* sheers away from the American Fast Combat Support Ship *Seattle* (AOE.3). Her low radar signature is to fool incoming SSMs as much as to avoid detection.**

La Fayette class, as built

Displacement: 3,200 tons (standard); 3,600 tons (full load)
Length: 115m/377ft 6in (bp); 124.2m/407ft 8in (oa)
Beam: 13.6m/44ft 8in
Draught: 4.8m/15ft 9in (maximum)
Armament: 1 x 100mm gun; 8 x MM40 Exocet SSM (2x4); 1 x 8-cell Crotale SAM launcher
Machinery: 4 diesel engines, 2 shafts
Power: 15,666kW/21,000bhp for 25 knots
Endurance: 350 tons fuel for 12,965km/7,000nm at 15 knots
Protection: Nominal
Complement: 153

LEFT: **A good beam shot of *Manju* of the Etorofu class, whose elegant destroyer-like hull belies her humbler status. Later units had hulls almost devoid of double-curvature plating. Her low-elevation 4.7in guns date from World War I.**

Shumushu and Etorofu classes

Although the Imperial Japanese Navy viewed convoy as "defensive" and, therefore, of low priority, it did produce during the late 1930s the four-strong Shumushu (or Shimushu) class of general-purpose escorts. Basically of sound design, they proved suitable for later series production and for further development. With some uncertainty as to their exact role, they were fitted initially for minesweeping.

Unlike the British and American navies, which disliked diesel propulsion (not least because it was then very noisy in an AS escort, which needed to minimize self-generated noise), the Japanese adopted it readily. Its advantages included compactness and few engine room staff, against which it required highly refined fuel, which would become difficult to obtain.

In length comparable with a British Castle-class corvette, a Shumushu was somewhat narrower, with a 3-knot speed advantage. Like a small destroyer, with no torpedo tubes, she had a very short forecastle which terminated short of the simple bridge structure, reminiscent of German World War I practice, illustrated elsewhere.

For their size, these escorts were relatively heavily gunned, i.e. with an eye to resisting surface attack rather than the threat from submarine and aircraft which actually developed. Both the Shumushus and the 14 virtually identical Etorofu type, that followed somewhat later, carried three single 4.7in guns, one forward, two aft. All were on low elevation mountings removed from destroyers scrapped after World War I.

As built, the early ships carried only a handful of automatic weapons and a dozen depth charges (without associated sound equipment) but, under pressure of combat experience, minesweeping gear

ABOVE: **The Etorofus (Type A) were the first derivative class, similar but of slightly greater displacement. This is *Kasodo* at an unknown date, fitted with a temporary bow, not an unfamiliar sight in the Pacific.**

and other topweight was landed in favour of up to 60 depth charges and a dozen or more 25mm automatic weapons. They also gained sonar and radar although, at this time, these were of indifferent quality.

ABOVE: **Although having the appearance of a wartime emergency design, the four Shumushus were completed pre-war. They were successful, and provided the basis for the extended classes of anti-submarine escorts that succeeded them.**

Etorofu class, as built

Displacement: 870 tons (standard); 1,020 tons (standard)
Length: 73m/239ft 7in (bp); 77.5m/254ft 4in (oa)
Beam: 9.5m/31ft 10in
Draught: 3.1m/10ft
Armament: 3 x 4.7in guns (3x1)
Machinery: Geared diesel engines, 2 shafts
Power: 3,133kW/4,200bhp for 19.5 knots
Endurance: 14,816km/8,000nm at 16 knots
Protection: None
Complement: 147

LEFT: **Where the earlier classes had been configured as general-purpose escorts with minesweeping gear, the Mikuras (Type B) were fitted primarily for AS duties. This is** *Awaji,* **early in 1944, with reduced surface armament and clear quarterdeck.**

Mikura and Ukuru classes

A major weakness of the Japanese high command was its inflexible attitude to planning so that, as the Pacific war developed into a protracted test of attrition, it was unwilling to adapt. Because a short war had been hypothesized, escorts came low on the construction priority list. This remained the case even when the Japanese merchant marine, upon which the sustenance of the newly acquired empire depended, was targeted by a growing infestation of American submarines. Thus, although the four Shumushus were launched in 1939–40, it would be late in

1942 before the first of the follow-on Etorofus entered the water. This class of 14 was then launched over a 14-month period with apparently little urgency even though, up to December 1943, over 2.9 million tons of mostly unconvoyed shipping had been lost.

From October 1943 the yet-incomplete Etorofu programme overlapped that for the eight Mikura type, modified and slightly enlarged. Their forecastles extended aft to the bridge block and the funnel was placed much farther aft. Although configured primarily for AS operations, with a 120

depth charge capacity and sonar gear, they were still burdened with three 4.7in guns, the after weapons in an open twin mounting. An interesting response to the lack of a purpose-designed, ahead-throwing weapon was to mount a 75mm Army-pattern mortar ahead of the bridge. Again, AA weaponry was augmented as opportunity offered.

The Mikuras, launched between July 1943 and February 1944, could be built in as little as six months. During this period, however, mercantile losses were causing some concern. The Mikura design was thus redrawn to cut out all complex, or double, curvature, even deck camber, in order to facilitate construction through the assembly of prefabricated modules. Thirty-three of these Ukuru-class variants were built.

ABOVE: **Later versions of the Mikuras were known as the Ukuru class, or Modified Type B. Of similar design, they began to incorporate single-curvature plating, as apparent in the bow section of the** *Ukuru* **herself, seen here post-war.**

Ukuru type, as built

Displacement: 940 tons (standard); 1,020 tons (full load)
Length: 72m/236ft 4in (bp); 78m/256ft (oa)
Beam: 9m/29ft 7in
Draught: 3.1m/10ft
Armament: 3 x 4.7in guns (1x2/1x1); 1 x 75mm mortar
Machinery: Geared diesel engines, 2 shafts
Power: 3,133kW/4,200bhp for 19.5 knots
Endurance: 9,260km/5,000nm at 16 knots
Protection: None
Complement: 150

LEFT: **Far too late, the Japanese began series production of escorts to screen their fast-diminishing merchant marine. The Kaibokans were smaller versions of the preceding classes. This example is a diesel-propelled Type C.**
ABOVE: **The Kaibokans were much smaller than Western AS escorts, and this unidentified Type D has succumbed quickly to the mining effect of several near missiles. As she rolls over, her crew can be seen evacuating.**

Kaibokan classes

Far too late, the Kaikobans were the major series-built, emergency escorts. They were known commonly as "Type C", Types "A" and "B" being the Shumushu/Etorofu and Mikura/Ukuru classes respectively. Although the "Type C" design was approved early in 1943, production began only late in that year. Despite its being given higher priority, the programme suffered from the generally poor organization and decision-making process that was a feature of a Japan unready for an extended war. There was a chronic lack of skilled workers and increasing shortages of essential, imported raw materials.

Types "A" and "B" were of about 78m/256ft overall length, their production confined to just five yards. The emergency Kaikoban programme involved an initial order of over 130 hulls. Many more yards needed to be involved, and it was probably to utilize smaller facilities that the "Type C" design was limited to 67.5m/221ft 6in. Less just one medium-calibre gun, however, they carried the same armament as the still-building "Type Bs".

Apparently too numerous to name, Kaikoban were simply numbered. With diesel engine production inadequate, some later units were given steam turbine propulsion. Twin-shaft, diesel-driven

ABOVE: **Due to a dearth of suitable diesel engines, the Type D Kaibokans were fitted with single-screw steam turbine machinery, evidenced by the smoke and taller funnel of this example, known simply as "No. 8".**

units (odd numbers) remained "Type C" but the slightly larger, single-shaft, turbine-driven ships (even numbers) were known as "Type Ds". Externally, these differed in having a taller, more slender funnel of round section, placed further forward than the hexagonal-sectioned stacks of the diesel ships.

Building times varied between three and eight months, and the programme was successful in that upwards of 90 units were definitively completed, many others existing as partly assembled modules. Although even the oldest saw barely a year of hostilities, it bears testimony to the, by then, overwhelming superiority of the Americans by sea

and air that 55 of them became war losses. Orders for hundreds more, many half-complete, were cancelled.

Type C, as built

Displacement: 745 tons (standard); 810 tons (full load)
Length: 63m/206ft 7in (bp); 67.5m/221ft 7in (oa)
Beam: 8.5m/27ft 10in
Draught: 2.9m/9ft 6in
Armament: 2 x 4.7in guns (2x1); 1 x 75mm mortar
Machinery: Geared diesel engines, 2 shafts
Power: 1,417kW/1,900bhp for 16.5 knots
Endurance: 12,040km/6,500nm at 14 knots
Protection: None
Complement: 136

LEFT: **This view of the** *Oi* **emphasizes the high forward freeboard of the Isuzu design. Anchors are partly recessed to reduce slamming and spray-making. Note the Bofors-type AB rocket launcher.**

Ikazuchi and Isuzu classes

Reconstructed as the Japanese Maritime Self-Defence Force (JMSDF), the Japanese navy was, during the early 1950s, permitted to build its first new ships. Closely controlling Japan's regeneration, the United States was also concerned at Soviet Russia's naval building in the Pacific. Japan's ability to defend herself, or even act as an ally, was to be encouraged.

A major perceived threat was from Russian high-speed conventional submarines, derived from captured German technology. These were capable of bursts of 15 to 17 knots submerged and, to engage them, it was reckoned that contemporary escorts needed to have a 10-knot speed advantage.

In December 1954 Japan laid down her first trio of new frigates. The Ikazuchis were smaller than the ex-American escorts that the JMSDF was already running, but showed the latter's influence in that armament and electronics were all American sourced. Unambitious, flush-decked vessels, they were armed with a pair of 3in guns, a Hedgehog and depth charges. There was a single, braced tripod mast, replaced by a lattice on the Isuzus.

All were twin-screwed, but *Akebono* (slightly the largest and with two funnels) was steam-turbine propelled, while the other single-funnelled pair had diesel engines, Mitsubishi in *Ikazuchi* and Mitsui/B&W in *Inazuma*.

Although the 28-knot *Akebono* was a clear 3 knots faster, she also required 30 more crew, and diesel propulsion was selected for the four Isuzus, launched in two pairs in 1961 and 1963. All four had differing types of diesel engine layout.

As long as a DE, but narrower, the Isuzu was an obvious derivative of the Ikazuchi, but differed in having fore- and mainmasts, both of lattice construction. Four 76mm/3in guns were carried, in twin mountings forward and aft. There was a forward-firing Bofors-type quadruple AS mortar and, later, AS torpedo tubes and VDS. They were very dependent upon standard American equipment but although capable, would have had difficulty in tackling a fast submarine.

LEFT: **Inheriting the name of a notable heavy cruiser of World War II, the** *Mogami* **shows her deck layout. Of an essentially simple design, suitable for series production, she carries her name amidships, a custom briefly revived post-war.**

Isuzu class, as built

Displacement: 1,490 tons (standard); 1,700 tons (full load)
Length: 94m/308ft 6in (oa)
Beam: 10.4m/34ft 2in
Draught: 3.5m/11ft 6in (mean)
Armament: 4 x 3in guns (2x2); 1 x quadruple AS mortar
Machinery: 4 diesel engines, 2 shafts
Power: 11,936kW/16,000bhp for 25 knots
Endurance: Not known
Protection: None
Complement: 180

Chikugo class

Developed Isuzus, the Chikugos followed after a lapse of seven years. They were slightly shorter, but beamier, continuing the trend to the deployment of increasingly sophisticated sensors and weaponry. From the Ikazuchis' already out-moded Hedgehog, the Isuzus tried the Americans Mk 108 launcher (Weapon Able) before adopting the Bofors quadruple mortar. With the Chikugos came ASROC, they being reputedly the smallest ships to carry it. Previous weapons had been forward-firing, and were located in "B" position, forward of the bridge. Depending upon sonar conditions, ASROC could range effectively to 9.6km/6 miles and could, therefore, be mounted aft of amidships

where its large Mk 16, 8-cell launcher was better protected, dominating the ship's profile. ASROC could deliver either a homing torpedo or a nuclear depth charge, although the latter are most likely never to have been supplied.

In layout, the Chikugos closely followed that of the Isuzus but, in overall appearance, had lost some of the latter's Japanese characteristics. The sharply cut-off funnel was replaced by a more conventional "flower-pot", while the traditional curved stem profile gave way to the heavily overhung, straight stem and anchor that advertised the bow-mounted sonar which necessarily complemented the ASROC. Later, the class would gain also a towed VDS,

located in a well in the transom, offset to starboard. In order to reduce wetness, the forward hull had a long knuckle, a feature then used extensively in the US Navy and, for designers, of debatable effectiveness.

Diesel propulsion was again specified and, once again, was sourced from two separate manufacturers. To reduce radiated noise, diesel engines were, by this time, being raft-mounted and supported on flexible mounts to decouple their noise and vibration from a ship's hull. AS torpedo tubes could also be shipped but, otherwise, the Chikugos were weakly armed.

All 11 were discarded between 1996 and 2003.

ABOVE: Lacking a helicopter for targeting, the *Chikugo*'s ASROC depended upon another ship or her own sonar to supply coordinates. A medium-frequency Variable Depth Sonar (VDS) is installed aft and a lower-frequency unit under the sharply raked bows.

Chikugo class, as designed

Displacement: 1,510 tons (standard); 1,760 tons (full load)
Length: 93m/305ft 3in (oa)
Beam: 10.8m/35ft 5in
Draught: 3.5m/11ft 6in (mean)
Armament: 2 x 3in guns (1x2); 1 x 8-cell ASROC launcher; 6 x 324mm AS torpedo tubes (2x3)
Machinery: 4 diesels, 2 shafts
Power: 11,936kW/16,000bhp for 25 knots
Endurance: 19,816km/10,700nm at 12 knots
Protection: Nominal
Complement: 165

LEFT: *Ishikari* was lead ship for a class of small multi-purpose frigates which, apparently, proved to be too small to meet their designated requirements. Note the Harpoon SSMs aft and a reversion to the Bofors pattern AS rocket launcher forward.

Ishikari and Yubari classes

By virtue of not being designed to operate shipborne helicopters, Japanese frigates tend to be small and compact but, by the standards of their peers, are more general-purpose combatants than specialist anti-submarine escorts. A Chikugo was less than half the displacement of, say, a British Type 23 but at 93m/305ft was obviously thought over-large, for the one-off *Ishikari*, launched in 1980, was a considerable 8.5m/27ft 10in shorter.

A consistent feature of Japanese frigates was a 25-knot maximum speed, achieved in the *Ishikari* with a Combined Diesel Or Gas (CODOG) turbine installation. Her two shafts are driven from a common gearbox, powered either by a single diesel (for cruising speeds up to 19 knots) or by a single, licence-built Olympus gas turbine. Although more compact, the arrangement lacks to a degree the versatility.

Externally, a major departure was to increase internal volume by the addition of a long, full-width deckhouse of an otherwise flush-decked hull. The bridge-mast-funnel arrangement is much the same, the large funnel casing resulting from the requirement of the gas turbine.

A considerable amount of aluminium alloy is reportedly incorporated in the upper structure. As such alloys can melt and fail in the event of a serious fire, this is not considered very good practice.

Apparently over-compact, the *Ishikari* was followed by the two Yubaris, near-identical but some 6.5m/21ft greater in length. Like her, their AS capability is limited to small-calibre torpedo tubes and a Bofors quadruple mortar. There is no bow sonar.

The gun calibre remains the same, but firepower is limited to a single weapon of OTO-Melara manufacture. A planned Vulcan/Phalanx CIWS appears never to have been fitted. There being no VDS, the low afterdeck is occupied by four to eight Harpoon SSMs.

LEFT: *Yubetsu* was the second of a pair of slightly enlarged Ishikari derivatives. The gearing arrangements were such that both shafts could be powered by either a single gas turbine or a single diesel engine.

Yubari type

Displacement: 1,470 tons (standard); 1,760 tons (full load)
Length: 91m/298ft 8in (oa)
Beam: 10.8m/35ft 5in
Draught: 3.6m/11ft 10in (mean)
Armament: 1 x 76mm gun; 4/8 x Harpoon SSM; 1 x quadruple 375mm AS mortar; 6 x 324mm AS torpedo tubes (2x3)
Machinery: 1 Olympus gas turbine and 1 diesel engine, 2 shafts
Power: 21,179kW/28,390shp for 25 knots or 3,730kW/5,000bhp for 19 knots
Endurance: Not known
Protection: Nominal
Complement: 98

Abukuma class

Terminated at just two units, the Yubari type was probably an exercise in producing a lean-crewed, small escort that could be series-built in an emergency. Too limited for peacetime activities, it was succeeded by the Abukuma class, six units that harked back to the earlier Chikugos.

The most important influence on the Abukumas was the decision to increase maximum speed to 27 knots. This required an increase in length, a full 16m/52ft 5in greater than that of a Chikugo. A necessary two-thirds increase in power is developed by a pair of Spey SM-1C gas turbines, whose size gives them a more economical operating range than the larger Olympus. For cruising, there are two diesel engines. Arranged CODOG-fashion, each shaft can be driven by one gas turbine or one diesel. The machinery is located in two, well-separated spaces, each served by a large, square-sectioned funnel.

The hull is of the long forecastle type, without a forward knuckle. The upper deck is continued right aft, over the short, open afterdeck. This gives the impression that the ships have both VDS and a helicopter pad. The former, however, is only a possible future option, while a helicopter can only be "vertically replenished" (VERTREP) while hovering.

The space between the funnels is occupied by an 8-cell ASROC launcher. ASROC rounds are now launched more

ABOVE: Unusual in modern frigates, the Abukumas have no shipborne helicopter. The area right aft, abaft *Chikuma*'s Phalanx CIWS, is fitted for the "vertical replenishment" (VERTREP) of helicopters, which have to remain on the hover. BELOW RIGHT: The large gap between *Chikuma*'s gun and the bridge front suggests that space has been reserved for the later addition of a small Vertical-Launch System (VLS). At present, ASROC is launched from an amidships Mk 112 mounting.

commonly from a Vertical Launch System (VLS). The considerable space between the bridge front and the gun suggests that a small VLS could well be another future option.

Ahead of the VERTREP area are two pairs of Harpoon SSMs and a Vulcan/Phalanx CIWS. Lack of a second CIWS and the usual complement of SSMs suggests topweight problems. The foremast is a truly massive lattice structure and there had yet appeared few concessions to radar invisibility.

Abukuma class, as built

Displacement: 2,050 tons (standard); 2,550 tons (full load)

Length: 109m/357ft 10in (oa)

Beam: 13.4m/44ft

Draught: 3.8m/12ft 6in (mean)

Armament: 1 x 76mm gun; 4 x Harpoon SSMs (2x2); 1 x 8-cell ASROC launcher; 1 x Vulcan/Phalanx CIWS; 6 x 324mm AS torpedo tubes (2x3)

Machinery: 2 gas turbines, 2 diesel engines, 2 shafts

Power: 20,142kW/27,000shp for 27 knots or 7,460kW/10,000shp for 19 knots

Endurance: Not known

Protection: Nominal

Complement: 115

ABOVE: *Oyodo* is seen fitted with two pairs of Harpoon SSMa aft, whereas *Chikuma* (top) has only empty cradles. It is now unusual for such small ships to be fitted with two funnels, whose black caps are something of a Japanese trademark.

LEFT: **Of 268 Rudderow type ordered, only 81 were actually completed, the programme being curtailed by the war's end. Compared with the Buckleys' 3in guns, the Rudderows' 5in 38 at either end look somewhat outsized.**

ABOVE: **No less than 152 Buckleys were completed, this being** *Wilmarth* **(DE.638). One of the "long-hull" types, the Buckleys accommodated machinery for a respectable 24 knots. Note the prominent trunking to the funnel and the triple-torpedo tubes, carried high.**

Destroyer Escort (DE) classes

As early as 1939 the US Navy was considering specifications for an escort vessel suitable for production in large numbers, which would release destroyers for the duties for which they had been designed. Protracted consideration of the conflicting merits of speed and armament, endurance and seakeeping indicated, however, that a larger number of standard destroyers would be better value.

A near-moribund project was then kick-started in June 1941 by an urgent request for escorts from a hard-pressed British Admiralty. All the necessary design work had been done for a small, destroyer-like vessel of some 91.5m/300ft overall, about the same size as a River-class frigate. Like British corvettes, these new "Destroyer Escorts", or DEs, would be built in yards not used to naval orders, although naval standards would apply.

The US Navy, now itself at war, realized the utility of DEs and the numbers involved became staggering. Over 1,000 were ordered, of which about 450 were eventually cancelled. Of 565 actually completed, 90 were transferred during hostilities, 78 of them to the Royal Navy.

The DEs' flush-decked hulls, with their pronounced forward sheer, were diminutives of those of American destroyers. The open-topped bridge, with its all-round visibility, was adopted from British practice. They were excellent seaboats but, designed with an unusually large metacentric height, they had a rapid and vicious motion until extra weight was moved topside and larger bilge keels fitted to dampen rolling.

US Navy practice stressed relatively high speeds, the DE's specification calling for steam turbines and 24 knots. With the numbers involved, machinery production could not keep pace, necessitating some

ABOVE: **DEs were transferred widely with the end of World War II, the French-flag** *Touareg* **being one of 14 acquired in two batches. One of the 21-knot diesel-electric Bostwick type, she served originally as the USS** *Bright* **(DE.747).**

units being diesel powered. Various combinations of machinery were used, resulting in six major variants of DE being recognized.

Experience with British Hunt classes had demonstrated the occasional value of torpedo tubes, and a triple bank was fitted to the Edsall, Buckley and Bostwick classes. In those transferred to the Royal Navy, all of the Evarts and Buckley types, the extra speed and tight turning circle were much appreciated (as were the relatively high-class accommodation and facilities). Although an excellent dual-purpose weapon, the 3in gun was considered by the British to be inadequate to quickly dispose of a surfaced submarine.

Type	Length (oa) (m/ft)	Beam (m/ft)	Propulsion type	Power (kW/h)	Speed (knots)	Armament
Evarts	88.3/289.5	10.7/35	Diesel-electric	4,476/6,000	21	3 x 3in
Edsall	93.3/306	11.3/37	Geared diesel	4,476/6,000	21	3 x 3in
Buckley	93.3/306	10.7/35	Turbo-electric	8,952/12,000	24	3 x 3in
Bostwick	93.3/306	10.7/35	Diesel-electric	4,476/6,000	21	3 x 3in
Butler	93.3/306	10.7/35	Turbo-electric	8,952/12,000	24	2 x 5in
Rudderow	93.3/306	10.7/35	Turbo-electric	8,952/12,000	24	2 x 5in

Two 3in guns were superimposed forward, "A" gun being very wet in a seaway. Abaft "B" gun was a full Hedgehog. Effective in its day, it proved to be the DE's weakness in that the highly efficient Squid (never adopted by the US Navy) could not be retro-fitted. The slower, but more roomy, British Lochs thus became the better U-boat killers.

The adoption of diesel drive was expedited by utilizing the standard 1,500hp diesel generator/motor combination already used in submarines. No less than eight of the sets were to have been installed to generate the required 12,000shp but, owing to conflicting demands of submarine and amphibious craft programmes, only four diesel engines per ship could be spared. Diesel-powered ships thus enjoyed only half the propulsive power of steamers, the speed penalty being 3 knots. In the Edsalls (only) diesels drove the shafts through gearing rather than electrically.

Post-war, 94 DEs were converted to high-speed transports (APDs), with accommodation for 162 troops and their equipment, with four LCVPs under davits. About 45 more became radar pickets, both types reflecting experience gained in the Pacific war. Many were transferred abroad post-war, some serving into the 1960s.

ABOVE LEFT: Resulting from the massed air attacks of World War II, the US Navy modified considerable numbers of destroyers and DEs to Radar Pickets for the purposes of providing early warning. *Calcaterra* (DER.390) was one of 34 Edsall-class conversions. ABOVE RIGHT: *Sellstrom* (DER.255) was another Edsall-class conversion. Note the full-width amidships deckhouse and modified bridge. She has been given an unshielded, twin 3in 50 forward and retains her Hedgehog, here uncovered. BELOW: During the south-west Pacific campaign, suitably modified "four-pipers", then DEs, proved to be invaluable as fast transports/troop carriers (APDs). *Ruchamkin* (APD.89) shows her assault landing craft and 5in gun for supporting fire.

LEFT: The diesel-electric *Dobler* (DE.48) of the short-hulled Evarts type was one of the original large British order that was retained by the US Navy. Two forward guns were appreciated, but at the cost of a very wet "A" position.

Buckley type, as built

Displacement: 1,400 tons (standard); 1,685 tons (full load)
Length: 91.5m/300ft (wl); 93.3m/306ft (oa)
Beam: 10.7m/35ft
Draught: 3.2m/10ft 6in (maximum)
Armament: 3 x 3in guns (3x1); 3 x 21in torpedo tubes (1x3); 1 x Hedgehog AS mortar
Machinery: Turbo-electric, 2 boilers, 2 shafts
Power: 8,952kW/12,000shp for 24 knots
Endurance: 11,112km/6,000nm at 12 knots
Protection: Nominal
Complement: 213

Dealey/Courtney and Claude Jones classes

Built to rigid standard specification in order to facilitate series production, DEs faced mass obsolescence by 1945 because of the rapid parallel advance of the fast, deep-diving submarine. As early as 1947, studies began for a DE replacement. Again, it had to be inexpensive and suitable for series production in an emergency.

A 27-knot speed, together with good seakeeping, demanded a hull of comparable dimensions. Because of the limited training angles of ahead-throwing weapons, a fast helm response and tight tactical diameter were important. In this respect, the US Navy favoured its Weapon Able (or Alfa) over the British Squid.

Based on the reasonable argument that wartime experience demonstrated that damaged ships survived by circumstance rather than by redundancy, single-screw propulsion was chosen, necessitating only one set of machinery and fewer personnel.

Not surprisingly, the indistinguishable Dealey and Courtney classes closely resembled earlier DEs, but with twin 3in 50s forward and aft, and a Weapon Able forward. A substantial lattice mast supported a comprehensive range of electronics, while much of the upper structure was in aluminium alloy. All 13 of the class were completed between 1954 and 1958, subsequent to the Korean War.

Some of the class were later converted to deploy the ultimately abortive DASH (Drone Anti-Submarine Helicopter) system but, even without this failure, they had been less than impressive with their high cost and insufficient range.

A long-forecastle, diesel-driven variant was thus developed in the four-ship Claude Jones class, completed 1958–60. These had four diesels, two shafts and two funnels. A 21.5 knot maximum was offset by an extra 1,852km/ 1,000nm endurance at the range of speed normally expected of a convoy

ABOVE LEFT: **Because of priorities in machinery production, many of the war-built DEs were powered for only 21 knots. They were, nonetheless, so valuable that the DE concept was updated post-war. This is the 25-knot *Courtney* (DE.1021).** ABOVE: **The post-war DE design proved to be useful for construction by allied NATO navies, the Portuguese building three Dealeys with mainly US offshore funding. *Almirante Gago Coutinho* has twin Bofors AS launchers in place of the usual Mk 108, Weapon "Able".**

escort. With very similar salient-dimensions, they had a reduced specification of two single 3in guns, two trainable Hedgehogs and two triple AS torpedo tubes. All four were transferred to Indonesia in 1973–74.

LEFT: **The four Claud Jones-class DEs were a post-war attempt to produce an inexpensive, diesel-driven escort. They proved to be too small and were transferred to Indonesia. This is the nameship *Monginsidi*. Note the two funnels.**

Dealey class, as built

Displacement: 1,450 tons (standard); 1,880 tons (full load)

Length: 93.9m/308ft (wl); 96.1m/325ft (oa)

Beam: 11.2m/36ft 8in

Draught: 3.7m/12ft

Armament: 4 x 3in (2x2); 1 x Able AS rocket launcher; 6 x AS torpedo tubes (2x3)

Machinery: Geared steam turbines, 2 boilers, 1 shaft

Power: 14,920kW/20,000shp for 25 knots

Endurance: 400 tons oil for 11,112km/6,000nm at 12 knots

Protection: Nominal

Complement: 173

Bronstein, Garcia and Brooke classes

With the introduction of the nuclear submarine came the requirement for a new type of escort, fast enough to be able to screen a task group, and capable of detecting and engaging a submerged target at a safe range. The key element for this was the low frequency SQS-26 sonar, necessarily housed in a large bulbous forefoot that required a telltale overhung bow profile.

The resulting sonar data would be used to control a Drone Anti-Submarine Helicopter (DASH). Theoretically, this could place a homing torpedo over a target at out to 9,144m/10,000yd but, proving unreliable, was effectively abandoned in 1968 in favour of the LAMPS (Light Airborne Multi-Purpose System) manned helicopter. This left the escorts with only ASROC, which had only half the range but which had the option of compensating for its lack of accuracy by carrying a nuclear warhead, capable of "sanitizing" a considerable area.

Completed in 1963, the two prototype Bronsteins were designed with

the smallest hull that could efficiently accommodate a SQS-26 system. Even powered with only 20,000shp, they were some 21.3m/70ft longer than earlier DEs. With adequate freeboard, their long forecastle-deck hulls did not require a pronounced forward sheer. A "mack" exhausted boiler uptakes via a plated-in mast and a generously dimensioned helipad was located about three-quarters aft. The 8-cell ASROC launcher was sited forward of the bridge.

The Bronstein design proved to be too tight and the derived Garica class were a further 13.1m/43ft longer. Guns were upgraded from four 3in to two 5in, the DASH facility being moved right aft. In the six-ship Brooke subgroup the

ABOVE LEFT: **The two Bronsteins (this is the *McCloy*) were the forerunners of a second-generation DE designed around the new ASROC stand-off missile. Larger and more expensive, they could target ASROC with both low-frequency bow sonar or helicopter-deployed sensors.** ABOVE: ***Albert David* (DE.1050) of the Garcia class executing a tight turn. Derived directly from the Bronsteins, the Garcias are significantly longer by virtue of shipping two 5in 38 guns and being equipped with a helicopter hangar, initially for the aborted DASH.** LEFT: ***Bronstein* (DE.1037) quietly proceeding at listening speed. The sheer size of her bow-mounted sonar dome requires her bower anchor to be stowed nearly abreast the 3in 50 gun mounting. Note that there is no hangar or ASROC reload facility.**

amidships 5in gun was exchanged for a modified Tartar SAM system. All had 35,000shp, but still with a single shaft. ASROCs were reloadable and heavy, wire-guided torpedoes could be launched through the transom.

ABOVE: ***Talbot* (FFG.4) was one of the six Garcia-class derivatives which exchanged the amidships 5in mounting for a Mk 22 launcher, intended for Standard SM-1 MR (Medium-Range) SSM.**

Garcia class, as designed

Displacement: 2,625 tons (standard); 3,480 tons (full load)
Length: 121.8m/400ft (wl); 126.3m/414ft 8in (oa)
Beam: 13.5m/44ft 3in
Draught: 7.9m/25ft 11in (maximum)
Armament: 2 x 5in guns (2x1); 1 x 8-cell ASROC launcher; 4 x AS torpedo tubes (2x2); 2 x 21in torpedo tubes (2x1)
Machinery: Geared steam turbine, 2 boilers, 1 shaft
Power: 26,110kW/35,000shp for 27+ knots
Endurance: 600 tons oil for 7,410km/4,000nm at 20 knots
Protection: Nominal
Complement: 209

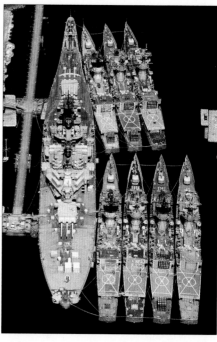

Knox class

The cost differential between the Tartar-armed Brooke-class DEGs and the non-missile, but otherwise similar, Garcia-class DEs was considerable and, for the planned successors, would be higher, To reduce unit cost in order to obtain the numbers required, the Knox-class ships did not receive an area defence SAM. Their programme overlapped that of the Garcias and, resulting from considerable effort to clean up the rather "bitty" appearance of earlier ships, they were reasonably handsome, if functional.

The truncated conical "mack" was located exactly amidships to minimize ship motion, bearing as it did a short lattice mast supporting the ships' electronics. Earlier classes carried

a stem anchor, with the second stowed, submarine-style, in the keel. The Knoxes were given a keel and a port-side anchor, the latter of Danforth pattern. It appears improbable that this feature created the wetness for which the class was noted, but both spray rails and bow bulwarks were added to most.

By the time that the lead ship entered service in 1969, DASH was a dead letter, the class being adapted for LAMPS. Its helipad was sited slightly forward of the after end and, to economize on length, was fitted with a telescopic hangar.

Much of the superstructure was made full width to increase internal volume. Forward was a 5in gun of the new, 54-calibre, type. The adjacent 8-cell ASROC launcher could be reloaded from a facility in the bridge front. Two cells were adapted to launch Harpoon SSMs as an option. Right aft, the originally fitted Sea Sparrow point-defence launcher was replaced by a single Vulcan-Phalanx CIWS. The large bow

ABOVE LEFT: **The Knox-class ships took the title "frigate" and designator "FF", FF.1054 being the** *Gray,* **seen here leading a Newport-class Tank Landing Ship. Her sonar dome, visible through the clear water, is smaller than those on preceding classes.** ABOVE: **The Knox class ran to 46 units, more than could usefully be employed in a peacetime navy, and many quickly found themselves reduced to reserve fleet status. Seven, showing remarkably few preservation measures, lay here alongside the veteran battleship** *New Jersey.*

sonar was complemented by VDS and/or towed array sonars.

The class extended to a respectable 46 units, all of which were disposed of by the mid-1990s. At the time of writing, a dozen or more are still serving under foreign flags.

LEFT: **The Knox class quickly acquired a reputation for wetness, and each was fitted with forward bulwarks and spray rail, as seen here on** *Aylwin* **(FF.1081). Note the CIWS added aft. Two cells of the ASROC launcher have been modified to launch Harpoon SSMs.**

Knox class, as designed

Displacement: 3,075 tons (standard); 4,070 tons (full load)
Length: 126.6m/415ft (wl); 133.6m/438ft (oa)
Beam: 14.3m/47ft
Draught: 7.6m/24ft (maximum)
Armament: 1 x 5in gun; 1 x 8-cell ASROC/Harpoon launcher; 1 x Sea Sparrow BPDMS; 4 x fixed AS torpedo tubes; 2 x fixed 21in torpedo tubes (2x1)
Machinery: Geared steam turbine, 2 boilers, 1 shaft
Power: 35,000shp/26,110kW for 27+ knots
Endurance: 750 tons oil for 8,100km/4,400nm at 20 knots
Protection: Nominal
Complement: 224

LEFT: **Derived directly from the Knox design, the Perrys differ in being built around a Standard/Harpoon system forward (relying on a single launcher) and facilities aft for a LAMPS-III helicopter and TACTASS towed array. They are classified "FFG".** BELOW: **Executing a zig-zag trials manoeuvre, *Kauffman* (FFG.59) shows her layout. Note the squat, round funnel casing exhausting the gas turbines, the single 76mm gun amidships and CIWS aft.**

Oliver Hazard Perry class

By 1970, the US Navy was faced with the mass retirement of modernized, war-built hulls. To maintain the required number of hulls, it appeared an attractive option to build "for but not with", creating a pool which could, at a later date, be fitted out specifically for AAW, ASW or surface warfare. The resulting 51 Perry-class missile frigates (FFG) were considerably upgraded Knoxes.

Procured under the strictest of cash-control regimes, the ships have a bow form capable of accepting a large Sonar,

LEFT: **The SM-1 version of the Standard SAM having reached retirement, the Perrys had the Mk 13 launcher removed, as in this photograph of *Elrod* (FFG.55). The newest 24 units are slated to receive an extensive modernization.**

which never materialized. The hull itself is Knox-like, but topped by a continuous, two-level boxy superstructure. Its after end extends full-width to provide a hangar for a pair of LAMPS-III, SH-60B Seahawk helicopters, not always carried. Their required operating area, however, necessitated the transom to be given a pronounced rake.

Because of the effectiveness of a double LAMPS-III, ASROC is not provided. All were fitted originally with a single-arm Mk 13 launcher forward, giving them "FFG" status. The launcher could handle Standard SM-1 MR SAMs or Harpoon SSMs. With the demise of the former in 2003, however, the launcher was removed. Not replaced with a VLS, the class has been down-graded to "FF" and 18 of the earlier units sold out to friendly flags.

Despite their capacious appearance, Perrys have little reserve capacity and are now up to 500 tons overweight. Despite this, they are criticized

(unreasonably) for their under-armed appearance, not helped by the adoption of a single 76mm OTO Melara for general-purpose firepower. Most have received a Vulcan Phalanx CIWS in addition. Some have their hull sonar complemented by a towed array.

The single shaft is driven by a pair of LM-2500 gas turbines, a pair of azimuth thrusters providing a measure of "get-you-home" redundancy.

A modernization programme for the 24 newest units has been proposed.

Earlier units, as designed

Displacement: 2,770 tons (standard); 3,660 tons (full load)
Length: 124.4m/408ft (wl); 135.7m/445ft (oa), or later 138.8m/455ft 7in (oa)
Beam: 15.2m/50ft
Draught: 8.6m/28ft 3in (maximum)
Armament: 1 x 76mm gun; 1 x standard SAM/Harpoon SSM launcher; 1 x Vulcan-Phalanx CIWS; 2 x AS torpedo tubes (2x1)
Machinery: 2 gas turbines (COGAG), 1 shaft
Power: 29,840kW/40,000shp for 29 knots
Endurance: 587 tons fuel for 7,730km/4,200nm at 20 knots
Protection: Splinter protection over vital spaces
Complement: 176 (now up to 225)

Spica class

The category of "torpedo boat", as opposed to "destroyer" was, as in the German Navy, only a matter of scale. Italian destroyers built during the early 1920s were of a maximum 876 tons and, being greatly outclassed by the 1,640-tonners of the mid-1930s, were downgraded to torpedo boats.

For the relatively short distances involved in Mediterranean operations, ships of this size were useful and, after over a decade's lapse, the 32-strong 800-ton Spica class were laid down from 1934. They resembled the contemporary Oriani-class fleet destroyers but could be quickly differentiated by their smaller, capped funnel, that of an Oriani being broad, trunked and not capped. The Italian love of 1930s streamlining was evident in the compact bridge structure and funnel being combined in a single entity, teardrop-shaped in plan.

They were not over-gunned, their three 100mm weapons being split between one on the forecastle and two superfiring aft. As built, some had four, sided 450mm torpedo tubes, each provided with a deck-mounted reload. Others had one centreline twin and two, sided reloadable tubes. During World War II all are believed to have had two twin centreline mountings. Heavily used as convoy escorts, particularly on the bitterly contested North Africa route, they were also fitted with shields on "A" and "Y" guns, their 20mm armament being increased to 16 barrels. They could carry up to 20 mines or their equivalent weight in depth charges.

LEFT: **One of the 16-strong Alcione type, *Libra* is seen here raising steam during World War II. Note the paravane, deployed by a powered davit. Three read-use depth charges are in the trap, while, forward of the canvas dodger, are two loaded throwers with reloads.**

ABOVE: ***Cassiopea* belonged to the Climene subgroup of the Spica class. She is seen here in the early 1950s, modified with a new bridge structure, as a "fast corvette". The attractive lines of her light destroyer pedigree remain in evidence.**

With twin-shaft, steam turbine propulsion, the Spicas could, with a clean hull and calm conditions, raise 34 knots but their speed fell off rapidly in the "deep and dirty" condition.

Two of the class were sold to Sweden in 1940 and 23 more were to become war losses. Survivors served as "fast corvettes" until the late 1950s, armed with Hedgehog but no torpedo tubes.

Spica class, as built

Displacement: 794 tons (standard); 1,020 tons (full load)
Length: 78.5m/257ft 8in (bp); 83.5m/274ft 1in (oa)
Beam: 8.1m/26ft 10in
Draught: 2.6m/8ft 6in
Armament: 3 x 100mm guns (3x1); 4 x 450mm torpedo tubes (4x1)
Machinery: Geared steam turbines, 2 boilers, 2 shafts
Power: 14,174kW/19,000shp for 34 knots
Endurance: 215 tons oil for 3,520km/1,900nm at 15 knots
Protection: None
Complement: 99

Ariete class

War estimates provided for no less than 42 Improved Spica, or Ariete, class torpedo boats. Italy's ability to carry through her emergency programmes was, however, already badly eroded and, by January 1942 when the first keel was laid, ten of the earlier class had already been lost. Only three yards were involved, all situated in the north and farthest removed from Allied interference. Despite this, only 16 had been laid down by September 1943, when Italy negotiated an armistice.

Ansaldo at Genoa had laid down its full six-ship allocation on the same day in July 1942. The two furthest advanced, *Ariete* and *Arturo*, were launched during March 1943, the former being delivered in the August. Ten more were launched and fitting out, but the *Ariete* would be the only one to serve in the Italian Navy.

Because of the remoteness of the yards from the battle front, the Germans succeeded in completing the remainder. They thus became war losses under the German flag. Only the *Ariete*, together with two damaged on the slip, survived the war, all three being ceded to the fleet of then-Yugoslavia.

The Arietes differed little from the original Spica class. The bridge front was squared-off rather than rounded. With

TOP: **The Italian port of Fiume was incorporated into post-war Yugoslavia as Rijeka. The incomplete hull of the *Balestra*, already renamed TA 47 by the Germans, was captured there. She was completed as the Yugoslav *Ucka* to a modified design.** ABOVE: **As the only unit of the class to be completed for the Italian Navy, the *Ariete* is seen here in the original form. Note the ungainly squared-off bridge structure and lack of main deck scuttles, as compared with *Ucka* (above).**

100mm guns in "A" and "X" positions only, and a larger, uncapped funnel, they could easily be confused visually with a fleet destroyer. A minesweeping winch and two sets of permanent minelaying rails were provided aft.

The main deck was no longer pierced for scuttles. This was probably a damage-control feature.

The class was officially referred to as "attack torpedo boats", a reference presumably to their two triple 450mm torpedo tube mountings and the 16 per cent increase in installed power, providing for a sustained sea speed of 31.5 knots.

Ariete class, as designed

Displacement: 757 tons (standard); 1,127 tons (full load)
Length: 81.1m/266ft 3in (bp); 83.5m/274ft 1in (oa)
Beam: 8.6m/28ft 3in
Draught: 3.1m/10ft 2in (mean)
Armament: 2 x 100mm guns (2x1); 6 x 450mm torpedo tubes (2x3)
Machinery: Geared steam turbines, 2 boilers, 2 shafts
Power: 16,412kW/22,000shp for 31.5 knots
Endurance: 214 tons oil for 2,780km/1,500nm at 16 knots
Protection: None
Complement: 150

LEFT: **Completed only shortly before the Italian capitulation, *Aliseo* survived only to be ceded to Yugoslavia. As can be seen, the Ciclone/ Animosos lowered the silhouette and landed "Y" gun for an increased depth charge capacity.**

Pegaso and Ciclone classes

A further variant of the Spica design was that of the four-strong Pegaso class. Although of much the same dimensions and appearance, the hulls were refined hydrodynamically for improved seakeeping and endurance. A small bulbous forefoot, common on Italian cruisers, was designed for optimal flow conditions over a specific speed band, allowing either higher speed for the same power, or greater economy at the same speed.

Instead of the Spicas' flattish cut-up, under the after end, typical of current destroyer practice, the Pegasos had a "cruiser" stern. Besides giving more buoyancy right aft, this would probably have given a more uniform flow over the propeller disc, reducing vibration and increasing propeller efficiency. Forward, a slight knuckle was introduced to reduce wetness. Very wet aft, the Spicas had a centreline catwalk connecting the forecastle deck to the light automatic

gun positions and "X" gun. On the Pegasos, the underside of this was filled in to create safe fore-and-aft access at upper deck level. Because of this, the two twin torpedo tube mountings had to be sided, halving the maximum salvo. Three depth charge projectors were provided on either side.

The 16 Ciclone-class "destroyer escorts" (*torpediniere di scorta*) were derived directly from the Pegasos.

LEFT: *Pegaso*, **one of four, has had a second depth charge trap added, forward of the propeller guard, allowing for larger patterns. The small crane, right aft, was a feature of these classes, and was provided to assist recovery of the paravanes.**

Mostly laid down before disruption and shortages bit too hard, most were completed before the armistice.

Looking similar to Pegasos but, in some cases, with a third 100mm gun added amidships, the Ciclones in general arrived too late to experience the worst of the North African convoy run. The only ones, therefore, to be lost in surface action with Allied forces were two of the three commandeered by the Germans following the separate Italian Armistice. With three being ceded to Soviet Russia and two to then-Yugoslavia none remained to Italy post-war.

Pegaso class, as designed

Displacement: 855 tons (standard); 1,600 tons (full load)
Length: 82.5m/270ft 1in (bp); 89.3m/293ft 2in (oa)
Beam: 9.7m/31ft 10in
Draught: 3.7m/12ft 2in (full load)
Armament: 2 x 100mm guns (2x1); 4 x 450mm torpedo tubes (2x2)
Machinery: Geared steam turbines, 2 boilers, 2 shafts
Power: 11,936kW/16,000shp for 28 knots
Endurance: 390 tons oil for 9,385km/5,100nm at 14 knots
Protection: None
Complement: 154

LEFT: **Already in an advanced state of completion, the Ciclone-class *Monsone* is seen here on the slip at Castellammare di Stabia. Note the adoption of a knuckle forward and the aftward extension of the forecastle deck.**

Albatros and de Cristofaro classes

In the early 1950s, the Italian Navy's escort forces comprised World War II survivors and three ex-American DEs, transferred under the Mutual Defence Assistance Programme. This last arrangement also funded Italy's first post-war corvettes, a series of eight providing much-needed employment.

Only three of these (the Albatros class) were to Italian account, four going to Denmark and one to the Netherlands. The Dutch, with limited use for a one-off, transferred theirs back to Italy after five years, when she was renamed *Aquila*.

Perhaps with a nod toward its source of funding, the Albatroses' hull abandoned the more usual Italian raised-forecastle

arrangement in favour of a flush-deck with a pronounced forward sheer. The compact superstructure was based on a full-width amidships deckhouse and there was a transom stern. No funnel was provided, the relatively low-power diesels exhausting through the hull.

Not much admired, the quartette were nonetheless useful 21-knot AS escorts, carrying two Hedgehogs and two 76mm guns (later replaced by 40mm weapons). Modest though they were, it would be seven years from their completion before Italy could embark on an improved version in the de Cristofaros, of which a fifth planned unit was cancelled.

About 4m/13ft longer, the hull of the de Cristofaros reverted to a raised forecastle design, the hance at the break of the forecastle being very long to increase the modulus at the hull discontinuity. A retained feature was the unusual "boat" bow profile. The higher-powered diesel engines exhausted through a small, tapered pot of a funnel. The two 76mm guns also gained a proper director.

The out-dated Hedgehogs and depth charges of the earlier class were here replaced by tripled AS torpedo tubes and a domestically developed, single-barrelled "Menon" AS mortar. VDS was added to a hull-mounted sonar.

ABOVE: **A decade later, but little larger, the four de Cristofaros were higher-powered and faster, with two improved 76mm guns and an Italian-designed Menon single-barrelled AS launcher in place of the Albatroses' two Hedgehogs. Note the reinstatement of a raised forecastle.**

de Cristofaro class

Displacement: 850 tons (standard); 1,020 tons (full load)
Length: 75m/246ft 2in (bp); 80.3m/263ft 7in (oa)
Beam: 10.3m/33ft 9in
Draught: 2.8m/9ft 2in
Armament: 2 x 76mm guns (2x1); 1 x 305mm Menon AS mortar; 6 x 324mm AS torpedo tubes (2x3)
Machinery: 2 diesel engines, 2 shafts
Power: 6,266kW/8,400bhp for 23 knots
Endurance: 100 tons fuel for 7,410km/4,000nm at 18 knots
Protection: None
Complement: 130

Centauro class

Also funded by the American mutual defence "offshore" programme were the four ships of the Centauro class. As ordered, they carried numbers from the US Navy DE series, starting with DE.1020, but, looking like destroyers, they took "D" pendant numbers on completion. With a speed of only 25 knots and no anti-surface ship torpedo tubes, however, they were later reclassified with "F" identifiers.

Although exceeding 1,800 tons displacement, they had features in common with the Albatros type, the hull being flush-decked, with a triangular, flat transom. Because of the greater length, the forward sheer did not appear to be so pronounced.

Since the early 1930s, Italian destroyers had been designed with adjacent boiler spaces and a single, large, trunked funnel. The arrangement was compact but vulnerable to a single hit. Since 1951, the Italians had been operating two ex-American destroyers. Their boiler spaces were separated for survivability, resulting in two funnels, with the Centauros following suit.

Forward and aft, the Centauros carried a totally new style of 76mm gun mounting, with two barrels arranged in a common vertical plane and elevating together. Although credited with a high rate of fire they proved to be over-complex and were replaced by a simpler single mounting.

Two paired 40mm mountings originally flanked the superfiring "X" position, their firing arcs reduced somewhat by the rather superfluous pole mainmast. Both mast and 40mm were latter suppressed in favour of a third 76mm gun.

In addition to an American-sourced sonar, there were two large-diameter AS torpedo tubes and depth charges, with a triple-barrelled Menon AS mortar in "B" position. This triple-barrelled version also proved to be relatively short-lived.

Not lending themselves easily to economical conversion to true AS frigates, the class began the process of disposal in 1980 with the sale of *Castore.*

ABOVE: **Modernization saw the Centauro class receive more orthodox single 76mm guns with proper director control. Further electronics tried the mast's stiffness, resulting in the addition of cross-bracing. Note that *Canopo*'s flag superior has been changed from "D" to "F".**

Centauro class, as designed

Displacement: 1,680 tons (standard); 2,120 tons (full load)
Length: 96.9m/317ft 8in (bp); 103.2m/338ft 4in (oa)
Beam: 11.6m/38ft
Draught: 3.5m/11ft 6in
Armament: 4 x 76mm guns (2x2); 2 x 21in torpedo tubes; 1 x 3-barrelled AS mortar
Machinery: Geared steam turbines, 2 boilers, 2 shafts
Power: 16,412kW/22,000shp for 25 knots
Endurance: 360 tons oil for 6,760km/3,650nm at 20 knots
Protection: None
Complement: 207

LEFT: *Alpino* (seen here) and her sister *Carabiniere* were developments of the Centauro design and, indeed, were originally to have taken "C" names. They have diesel engines of far higher output than their predecessor's steam plant, two helicopters and six 76mm guns.

ABOVE: The four Bergaminis show a different and cheaper line of development from the Centauro design. They have two 76mm guns and a mortar forward, like the Alpinos, but just one helicopter and half the engine power. This is *Luigi Rizzo*.

Carlo Bergamini and Alpino classes

Launched in 1960, the four Bergaminis were frigate versions of the de Cristofaro corvettes. For an extra 10m/33ft, they shipped a helicopter and a third gun, and gained 2.5 knots.

Again, a flush-decked hull was topped with a full-width deckhouse, now supporting at its after end a telescopic hangar for a small Agusta-Bell 47 helicopter. A light, elevated extension of the 01 level served as a flight pad. Active fin stabilizers were fitted to assist flight operations through roll reduction.

During the late 1960s, helicopter facilities were upgraded for the more capable AB.212. A larger hangar and extended flight pad meant the landing of the after 76mm guns and a single-barrelled Menon AS launcher. The uptakes from the four diesels exhausted via a funnel/mast combination. Beyond further upgrading, the Bergaminis were discarded in the early 1980s.

Some 20m/65ft 7in longer than the Bergaminis, the two Alpinos took the concept a stage further. This pair were to have been named *Circe* and *Climene*, continuing the astronomical names associated with torpedo boats. Before launch, however, they took *Alpino* and *Carabiniere*, old destroyer names that better reflected their size.

Their propulsion was by two small gas turbines and four diesels in CODAG combination. The resulting large funnel had proportions which greatly enhanced the ships' appearance. To the usual Menon launcher and two 76mm guns mounted forward were added four more 76mms, sided along the superstructure. Accommodation, originally for two small AB 204B helicopters, was later adequate for a single AB.212.

Two further units were cancelled but both Alpinos still exist (at the time of writing) as special-purpose auxiliaries and trials ships. They have been reduced to diesel propulsion only and their armament cut to three guns and their helicopter. Both now carry "A", auxiliary pendant numbers.

Alpino class, as designed	

Displacement: 2,000 tons (standard); 2,690 tons (full load)

Length: 106.4m/349ft 3in (bp); 113.3m/371ft 10in (oa)

Beam: 13.3m/43ft 8in

Draught: 3.8m/12ft 5in

Armament: 6 x 76mm guns (6x1); 1 x single-barrelled AS mortar; 6 x 324mm AS torpedo tubes (2x3)

Machinery: 2 gas turbines, 4 diesels, 2 shafts

Power: 11,488kW/15,400hp plus 12,533kW/16,800bhp for 28 knots

Endurance: 275 tons fuel for 7,780km/4,200nm at 17 knots

Protection: Nominal

Complement: 247

ABOVE: Lead ship *Carlo Bergamini* in historic surroundings. Her small helicopter is demanding on space, which has been economized by the combination of mast and funnel, and a telescopic hangar. The flight pad is well forward to minimize movement and accelerations.

LEFT: **With massive gas turbine sprint power in a relatively small hull, the Lupos had an un-frigate-like 35-knot top speed, but cruised on diesel engines.** *Sagittario*'s **four starboard-side Otomat SSM cradles are unoccupied.**

Lupo and Artigliere classes

Although of the same length as the preceding Alpinos, the Lupos, most unusually, were significantly narrower. The reason, probably, lay in the adoption of CODOG (as opposed to CODAG) propulsion. Two diesel engines were installed for cruising (up to 20 knots) but, for sprint power, there were two licence-built LM-2500 gas turbines, capable of a joint 37,300kW/50,000hp output. This represented a 25 per cent increase in propulsive power compared with an *Alpino*, and which, with an improved hull form, translated into a 4-knot increase in sustained speed.

Some sacrifice was necessary in topweight and a single 127mm gun,

and tube- and helicopter-launched torpedoes were able to replace the earlier six 76mm weapons and Menon AS launcher, now obsolete. Modern missile systems are bulky but not heavy, the Lupos carrying both an 8-cell Sea Sparrow point defence SAM and eight canister-launchers for Otomat SSMs.

That the Lupo design was too tight was evident in the class being curtailed in favour of the longer Maestrale type, all being scrapped by 2003. Handsome ships, they sold well for export, however, with six being built to Venezuelan account and four each to Peru and Iraq. The last named, laid down 1981–84, ran foul of a generally imposed embargo

on West-supplied war materials. With no potential buyers, they were taken into the Italian Navy as the Artigliere class.

All remain on the inventory and are effectively identical with the late Lupo class, with the important difference that acceptance was conditional upon all ASW weaponry and sensors being removed. This was presumably a budgetary manoeuvre, the ships being officially "Fleet Patrol Ships" rather than frigates. To compensate for their lack of ASW armament (which, presumably, could be added), their helicopters have enhanced capability for over-the-horizon direction for the ships' SSMs.

LEFT: **Between 1980 and 1982, Italy completed six standard Lupos for Venezuela. Here, the** *Mariscal Antonio José de Sucre* **crosses the stern of the stationary** *General Bartolomé Salom.* **Both are carrying their full outfit of Otomat SSMs.**

Lupo class, as designed

Displacement: 2,210 tons (standard); 2,525 tons (full load)
Length: 106m/347ft 11in (bp); 113.6m/372ft 10in (oa)
Beam: 12m/39ft 4in
Draught: 3.5m/11ft 7in
Armament: 1 x 127mm gun; 8 x Otomat SSM (8x1); 1 x 8-cell Sea Sparrow SAM launcher; 6 x 324mm AS torpedo tubes (2x3)
Machinery: 2 gas turbines, 2 diesels, 2 shafts
Power: 37,300kW/50,000hp or 5,968kW/8,000bhp for 35 or 20 knots
Endurance: 8,060km/4,350nm at 16 knots
Protection: Nominal
Complement: 194

Maestrale class

The limitations of the Lupo design were recognized early, for the first half-dozen of the improved version, the Maestrales, were ordered nine months before the lead ship, *Lupo*, even commissioned. Although 10m/33ft longer, they were even finer (L/B *Lupo* 8.83; *Maestrale* 9.04) and further reduction of weapon topweight was evident. A Lupo's Sea Sparrow launcher and its director were mounted on the hangar roof at 02 level. On a Maestrale the launcher has been moved to 01 level, superfiring the 127mm gun from "B" position. The compact Italian-built RTN-30X director above the bridge serves both weapons. A Lupo carried eight Otomat SSMs at 01 level. A Maestrale carries only four, in a less cramped 02 location, a net gain offset by the shift of the two twin 40mm mountings from main deck to 01 level.

The small increase in beam allowed the hangar to be widened sufficiently to accommodate a second helicopter. For ASW, these work in conjunction with the ships' VDS and towed array, deployed from a handling deck and well situated beneath the flight deck.

Although rather more powerful cruising diesels are fitted, higher speeds remain dependent upon a pair of LM-2500 gas turbines. Given the greater length it is, perhaps, surprising that they are credited with being upwards of 2 knots slower than a Lupo.

It is reported that the Maestrales were designed with no capacity for mid-life modernization and that their retirement is planned for 2011–15. The planned replacement for both the Maestrales and the already defunct Lupos is a new ten-ship class of general-purpose frigate, the lead ship of which will be named, rather

ABOVE LEFT: **Easily mistaken for a Lupo (opposite), a Maestrale differs primarily in having her SAM launcher forward of the bridge and in having a distinct gap between funnel casing and mainmast. This is** *Libeccio*. ABOVE: **This overhead view of** *Maestrale* **emphasizes the complexity of the modern funnel, whose contents are critical to the functioning of the ship's gas turbines as well as exhausting the cruising diesels and auxiliaries. It needs to be carefully cooled.**

confusingly, *Carlo Bergamini*. At 5,000 tons displacement and 135m/443ft 2in overall length, these will mark a considerable advance in size, capability and adaptability. They will be similar to the projected French Aquitaine class.

LEFT: **In the later stages of fitting out,** *Grecale* **presents her unusual stern configuration. The transom, very wide to support the helicopter deck above, is deeply notched to facilitate deployment of the variable depth sonar.**

Maestrale class, as designed

Displacement: 2,700 tons (standard); 3,040 tons (full load)
Length: 116.4m/382ft 1in (bp); 122.7m/402ft 10in (oa)
Beam: 12.9m/42ft 4in
Draught: 6m/19ft 6in (maximum)
Armament: 1 x 127mm gun; 4 x Teseo/Otomat SSM (4x1); 1 x 8-cell Aspide/Sea Sparrow SAM launcher; 2 x 533mm AS torpedo tubes (2x1); 6 x 324mm AS torpedo tubes (2x3)
Machinery: 2 gas turbines, 2 diesels, 2 shafts
Power: 37,300kW/50,000hp or 7,572kW/10,150bhp for 33 or 21 knots
Endurance: 11,110km/6,000nm at 15 knots
Protection: Nominal
Complement: 225

LEFT: **Rather like a cut-down Maestrale in appearance, the *Minerva* differs in having a low afterdeck not overlaid with the helicopter flight pad. The practice of painting discharge areas black gives a rather tatty appearance.** ABOVE: ***Fenice* is seen here with the original lower funnel, which affected helicopter operation. The latter's pad has been moved forward to reduce the effect of ship motion, itself reduced by active stabilizers.**

Minerva class

Classed officially as "light frigates" (FFL), the Minervas, slightly larger than a torpedo boat (light destroyer) of World War II, are configured as general-purpose escorts. Their hulls have relatively high freeboard and are of long forecastle type with a knuckle forward. Although the bridge structure is of full width, it is not elongated as in earlier classes. Forward is a single 76mm OTO-Melara Super Rapid gun, a dual-purpose weapon supported by an 8-cell Sea Sparrow/Aspide SAM launcher, a point-defence weapon that occupies premium space on the low afterdeck. Standard AS capability is thus limited to small-calibre torpedo tubes and a keel-mounted sonar. Space, however, has been allocated for the addition of a VDS.

Conflicting priorities are evident in that four units have landed their SAM system and torpedo tubes in favour of a projected helicopter facility. A helicopter and VDS would greatly enhance the AS qualities of the ships, but at the expense of self-defence (or that of any vessel under escort).

A further designed option is to ship both SAM system and a reload facility, together with four Otomat/Teseo SSMs, giving flexibility for fitting out according to likely operational requirements.

Between 2002 and 2004 were completed six more corvettes classed, probably for funding purposes, as patrol ships (Sirio class) or EEZ patrol ships (Fulgosi class). Built on a common, 88.4 x 12.2m/290 x 40ft hull, they are slightly longer than a Minerva but proportionately beamier. Their hulls follow contemporary fashion, with highly sculpted, low-signature features. As patrol vessels, most have a reduced armament.

Where the Sirio type is powered for only 22 knots, the Fulgosis are as fast as a Minerva (although requiring 58 per cent more installed power due to a fuller hull form). Both types already carry a 76mm gun and facilities (with telescopic hangar) for a large helicopter.

Minerva class, as designed

Displacement: 1,030 tons (standard); 1,285 tons (full load)
Length: 80m/262ft 7in (bp); 86.6m/284ft 3in (oa)
Beam: 10.5m/34ft 6in
Draught: 4.8m/15ft 9in (maximum)
Armament: 1 x 76mm gun; 1 x 8-cell Aspide/ Sea Sparrow SAM launcher; 6 x 324mm AS torpedo tubes (2x3)
Machinery: 2 diesel engines, 2 shafts
Power: 8,206kW/11,000bhp for 25 knots
Endurance: 6,480km/3,500nm at 18 knots
Protection: Nominal
Complement: 133

ABOVE: **Like most of the class, *Urania* is operating without either helicopter or Aspide/Albatros launcher which, if shipped, are alternatives. The ships are at the low end of displacement to effectively operate either.**

Kola class

Designed shortly after World War II, the Kola-class fast escorts remained on the active list until the late 1970s. Between six and ten were built, their design borrowing features from German fleet torpedo boats (light destroyers), particularly the T25–36 group of 1941–42, commonly known as Elbings, and of much the same size. The low-set, spray-deflecting knuckle forward was typically German, as was the configuration of the wide transom stern. The latter was specifically to facilitate the laying of mines, tracks for which extended on either side as far as the forward funnel.

The profile of a Kola was pleasing, with two single 100mm guns in open mountings superimposed at either end. Two well-separated, strongly raked and capped funnels indicated boiler spaces

divided by the engine room. Between the funnels was a centreline, triple torpedo tube mounting. Grouped around the after funnel were four twin automatic gun mountings, two of 37mm, two of 25mm. That most units appeared to lack two of these, together with the usual MBU AS rocket launchers, reinforced the general suspicion that the design was rather tender. Certainly, the dangers of ice accretion and extreme weather were avoided by assigning the class generally to the Black Sea fleet.

The length of the permanent mine rails suggested a capacity of at least 80. This considerable extra load could have been accepted only at the expense of landing other armament to compensate.

A feature of the main gun disposition was the lack of protection for the crews

ABOVE: **With the Soviet system then at its most secretive, good photographs of Kolas are scarce, identities of individual vessels rendered uncertain through change of pendant numbers. The Kolas' light armament classed them as "escorts" rather than destroyers.**

of "A" and "Y" guns, exposed to the muzzle blast from "B" and "X" guns.

The comparatively large, enclosed bridge structure was topped by a heavy "Wasp Head" director (derived from the stabilized German "Wackeltopf") to the front of which was attached the "Sun Visor" radar antenna. Only one triple 21in mounting was ever fitted.

LEFT: **Although heavily retouched, this image of a Kola shows her major features, particularly the long, unobstructed side decks and wide transom associated with minelaying. The flush deck reduces stress concentrations in the hull.**

Kola class, as designed

Displacement: 1,500 tons (standard); 1,900 tons (full load)
Length: 96m/315ft 2in (oa)
Beam: 10.4m/34ft 2in
Draught: 3.5m/11ft 6in
Armament: 4 x 100mm guns (4x1); 3 x 21in torpedo tubes (1x3); 2 x quadruple MBU-900 AS rocket launchers
Machinery: Geared steam turbines, 2 boilers, 2 shafts
Power: 22,380kW/30,000shp for 30.5 knots
Endurance: 300 tons oil for 6,480km/3,500nm at 12 knots
Protection: Not known
Complement: 190

Riga class

With more the characteristics of destroyers than the escorts that were required, the Kolas were too much configured for speed and insufficiently for capacity. Their programme was thus curtailed in favour of the Riga, a more frigate-like type whose design was, in many respects, a reduced Kola.

Overall length was reduced by 4.5m/14ft 9in, but the beam was little changed. By accepting a 28 knot (as opposed to 30.5 knot) speed, installed power could be reduced by one third. The shorter hull required the boilers to be located in adjacent spaces, reducing survivability but requiring only one large funnel to exhaust both.

Although it retained the broad, minelayer's transom, the Riga hull already showed more "Russian"

characteristics, flush-decked with a long, sweeping sheerline, the anchor pocket set well back. There was no knuckle but an enhanced flare. To further reduce wetness, a short bulwark was added right forward and an American-style, full-width screen abreast "B" gun. A solid bulwark ran from the screen to the funnel; with the 01 level continued to the ship's sides, this created a covered way.

Three 100mm guns were fitted, two superimposed forward, one aft at upper deck level. Two MBU AS rocket launchers, of various types, flanked "B" mounting at 01 level. Immediately abaft the funnel was a triple torpedo tube mounting. Permanent rails ran along either side as far forward as the funnel, their capacity about 50 mines if the tubes were landed as partial compensation.

ABOVE: **Finland acquired two Rigas from the Soviet Union in 1964. This is the *Hameenmaa*. Note the height of the 100mm guns in their trunions, indicating high elevation angles.**

Originally fitted with braced tripod masts, Rigas eventually gained a lattice structure to support increased electronic equipment.

Roughly equivalent to a British Hunt, the Riga proved to be rugged and seaworthy. Sixty-six were reportedly built, of which sixteen were transferred to including states from Finland to Indonesia. Some, fitted for intelligence gathering, gained a stub mainmast. All were discarded by the late 1980s, some having served for over 30 years.

ABOVE: **In an attitude typical of the Cold War era, the Wasp Head director and "A" gun of this unidentified Riga are tracking the photographer's aircraft, although the gun crews are not closed up. Note the broad transom and clear side decks. The funnel casing is louvred to direct gases away from the electronics.**

Riga class

Displacement: 1,080 tons (standard); 1,400 tons (full load)

Length: 91.5m/300ft 4in (oa)

Beam: 10.1m/33ft 2in

Draught: 3.3m/10ft 10in

Armament: 3 x 100mm guns (3x1); 3 x 21in torpedo tubes (1x3); 2 x MBU-2500 AS rocket launchers

Machinery: Geared steam turbines, 2 boilers, 2 shafts

Power: 14,920kW/20,000shp for 28 knots

Endurance: 230 tons oil for 4,075km/2,200nm at 15 knots

Protection: Not known

Complement: 177

LEFT: **Designed for coastal escort duties, this Petya I shows her broad range of armament: two enclosed twin 76mm gun mountings, two shrouded MBU-2500 AS rocket launchers forward of the bridge and two aft, and a covered quintuple torpedo tube bank amidships.** ABOVE: **An interesting close-up of a Petya fitted with two of the later MBU-2500A AS weapons. The bowl over the bridge is the Hawk Screech fire control radar for the 76mm guns. The casual "rig of the day" suggests that she is a Black Sea unit.**

Petya and Mirka classes

Produced in parallel with the Poti programme were 46 of the larger and more capable Petya class. Multi-role craft, they were triple-screwed, the centreline shaft being driven by two cruising diesels, and each wing shaft by a gas turbine. The hull was flush-decked, with marked forward sheer and a forward bulwark. Mine rails terminated at the broad transom.

As designed, Petyas had an enclosed twin 76mm gun mounting forward and aft, a quintuple 400mm AS torpedo tube bank abaft the low, square stack, and four of the flat-form MBU-2500s AS rocket launchers. Two of these were located aft and two on the bridge structure in a position that appeared perilously close to the wheelhouse windows.

Later units, known as Petya IIs, exchanged the after MBU-2500s for a second quintuple torpedo tube mounting, the bridge-mounted launchers being upgraded to the round-form MBU-2500-A.

A third variant, known variously as a Modified Petya I, or a Petya III, landed the after torpedo tubes in favour of various configurations of deckhouse, enclosing a VDS.

Of virtually the same size as a Petya, the succeeding Mirka varied mainly in its propulsion system. Two shafts were each usually powered by a cruising diesel engine. The propellers ran in tunnels, configured to as to act also as water jets when powered by the alternative gas turbines. The latter

were housed, Poti-style, in the raised after end of the hull. Lacking a funnel, the Mirka had their lattice mast relocated amidships to minimize motion.

The raised after end prevented Mirkas being mine-capable, but two MBU-2500-As were sided both forward and aft. A Mirka II variant, however, exchanged the after pair for a second quintuple set of torpedo tubes. Nine of each type were constructed.

Some Petyas were transferred, but no Mirka. Units of both classes served into the 1990s.

Mirka II

Displacement: 950 tons (standard); 1,120 tons (full load)
Length: 78m/256ft (bp); 82.4m/270ft 6in (oa)
Beam: 9.2m/30ft 2in
Draught: 2.9m/9ft 6in
Armament: 4 x 76mm guns (2x2); 10 x 400mm AS torpedo tubes (2x5); 2 x MBU-2500-A AS rocket launchers
Machinery: 2 gas turbines, 2 diesel engines, 2 shafts
Power: 22,380kW/30,000shp for 33 knots or 8,952kW/12,000bhp for 20 knots
Endurance: 150 tons fuel for 5,555km/3,000nm at 20 knots
Protection: None
Complement: 92

ABOVE: **Successors to the Petyas, the Mirkas had their gas turbines relocated right aft. Note the raised deckline and large air intakes. This is a Mirka II, with two quintuple torpedo tubes but no MBUs aft.**

LEFT: **A slightly confusing picture with the two Potis overlapping. Their flat 16-barrelled MBU-2500 projectors are also staggered, the forward one to port, the superimposed one to starboard. The hump over the gas turbine space is even more pronounced.**

Poti class

Although, in the early 1960s, Soviet Russia posed an enormous threat to the West through its considerable submarine fleet, the Russians themselves faced a similar threat. This ranged from nuclear attack boats, and SSBNs deploying the Polaris ICBM, to conventional diesel-electric boats, and resulted in a range of specialist Russian ASW vessels, varying in size from large helicopter carriers to corvette-sized craft designed for inshore AS operations.

Smallest of the latter type, and surely among the least attractive warships of all time, were the Poti class. Slightly smaller than a British Flower-class corvette of World War II, the Potis had CODAG propulsion with two diesel engines ahead, and two small gas turbines. Each drives a separate shaft, partly enclosed within tunnels. With all four engines coupled, the top speed was probably nearer 30, rather than the 34 knots sometimes claimed. The latter figure appears excessive for a small, non-planing hull.

Otherwise flush-decked, with marked sheer, the hull had a raised after section to accommodate the air ingestion units for the gas turbines, whose large, shrouded intakes were arranged in tandem. An unintentional bonus was that the odd profile made it, from a distance, difficult to estimate the ship's heading.

On two levels forward, and staggered about the centreline, were two MBU-2500A AS rocket launchers. Looking outsize on so small a ship, these could lay six-or-twelve bomb salvoes out to about 6.4km/4 miles' range. In the waist, firing outboard at fixed angles to the centreline, were four long, medium-calibre tubes for the launching of wire-guided AS torpedoes.

For self-defence a Poti depended upon the radar-directed, twin 57mm mounting amidships.

Over 60 Poti were believed built, several being transferred within the Warsaw Pact navies. Most served well into the 1980s.

ABOVE: **With its darkly painted after end, this Poti looks distinctly ungainly, but paint schemes varied from ship to ship. Visible amidships is the twin 57mm gun mounting with its associated Muff Cob director. To its left can be seen the two starboard 400mm torpedo tubes.**

Poti class

Displacement: 530 tons (standard); 615 tons (full load)

Length: 60.7m/199ft 3in (oa)

Beam: 8.2m/26ft 11in

Draught: 2.9m/9ft 6in

Armament: 2 x 57mm guns (1x2); 4 x 400mm AS torpedo tubes (4x1); 2 x MBU-2500-A AS rocket launchers

Machinery: 2 gas turbines, 2 diesel engines, 4 shafts

Power: 17,904kW/24,000shp plus 5,968kW/8,000bhp for 30+ knots

Endurance: 125 tons fuel for 4,815km/2,600nm at 16 knots

Protection: None

Complement: 80

LEFT: **At about 71.5m/234ft 7in, a Grisha lies somewhere between a Poti and a Mirka, but is a much neater design. This unit, the Lithuanian-flag *Aukstaitis*, was one of two acquired from Russia in 1992. Note the NATO-style number.** ABOVE: ***Aukstaitis* again. This variant is termed a Grisha III, which appears to vary only in the addition of a six-barrelled, Gatling-type 23mm gun, whose helmet-like containment is visible between the after 57mm gun mounting and its director.** BELOW: **A late-model Grisha V. The circular cover on the forecastle screens a "pop-up" SA-N-4 ("Gecko") SAM launcher, whose control is through the Pop Group director atop the bridge. Her main surface/air search radar is an updated Half Plate-B.**

Grisha class

At around 1,000 tons full load displacement, the Grishas are considered corvettes. They were built in considerable numbers, probably about 70 in all. While they were follow-ons to the Poti class, they are 11m/36t longer and constitute a new design rather than a derivative.

The hull has the same pronounced sheerline, but here flattened somewhat right forward to allow any forward guns to depress. The bridge structure is based on a full-width deckhouse, abaft which is a low, square-sectioned funnel, offset slightly to port and exhausting both the gas turbine and the two diesels of the CODAG propulsion system. Broad after waterplanes permit mine rails to run along either side from the after superstructure to the wide transom.

Grishas are, depending upon armament fit, divided into several sub-types. Grisha I had a retractable SA-N-4 ("Gecko") twin SAM launcher on the foredeck, superfired by two MBU-6000 12-barrelled AS rocket launchers. Sided in the waist were twin heavyweight torpedo tubes, and aft there was a twin 57mm gun mounting. Grisha IIs differed in having a second twin 57mm forward in place of the SA-N-4. All surviving examples of Types I and II reportedly serve with the Federal Border Guard in its large quasi-military fleet.

Grisha IIIs replicate Type Is but have a modified after deckhouse, which accommodates a VDS system and supports a six-barrelled 30mm Gatling. Grisha IVs appear never to have existed, the follow-ons being Grisha V. Probably 20 of these are still active. They have improved electronics while, aft, the twin 57mm mounting has been replaced by a single 76.2mm. Only one MBU-6000 is carried forward, indicating possible topside weight limitation.

The defensive firepower of all surviving Grishas has been augmented significantly by their being equipped with shoulder-launched Strela-3 close-range SAMs. Despite considerable variation, the Grisha classes are collectively termed MPK, an acronym for "Small AS Ship".

Grisha V

Displacement: 880 tons (standard); 1,030 tons (full load)
Length: 66.9m/219ft 4in (wl); 71.2m/233ft 5in (oa)
Beam: 9.5m/31ft 2in
Draught: 3.6m/11ft 9in
Armament: 1 x 76.2mm gun; 1 x 6-barrelled 30mm Gatling; 1 x SA-N-4 twin SAM launcher; 2 x shoulder-launched SA-N-8; 4 x 533mm torpedo tubes (2x2); 1 x MBU-6000 AS rocket launcher
Machinery: 1 gas turbine, 2 diesels, 3 shafts
Power: Gas turbine 13,428kW/18,000shp; diesels 7,460kW/10,000bhp each; total CODAG configuration 28,348kW/38,000shp for 32 knots
Endurance: 143 tons fuel for 4,630km/2,500nm at 14 knots
Protection: Nominal
Complement: 86

Krivak class

Powerfully armed for their size and often categorized as "destroyers", the Krivaks were built for the Soviet Navy as "large anti-submarine ships" and are, therefore, more correctly frigates.

The Krivak hull is of long forecastle type, with adequate freeboard. A slight knuckle over the centre section results from a gentle flare at the waterline. The sharply overhung stem betokens provision for a large bow sonar. On the low afterdeck a centreline casing covers a VDS, flanked by the usual mine rails.

The bridge structure is sited to place both it and the major electronics close to amidships, to minimize the effects of ship motion. The foredeck is dominated by a quadruple SS-N-14 ("Silex") launcher. This missile is dual purpose, capable of being fitted to carry either warhead or torpedo, for use against surface ship or submarine out to a 50km/31 mile range. With no embarked helicopter, the ship may require assistance in targeting.

Forward and aft are the unobtrusive silos for the pop-up SA-N-4 ("Gecko") launcher. Each has its own director. Forward of the bridge are the usual pair of MBU-6000 AS rocket launchers, while at the break of the forecastle deck are superimposed gun mountings, twin 76.2mm in Krivak Is and single 100mm in Krivak IIs. Forward of the stumpy funnel is a square deckhouse supporting radar directors for both the guns and the after SA-N-4. Sided abreast the amidships gap are quadruple heavyweight torpedo tubes. Propulsion is by gas turbine, cruise and boost units being run in COGAG configuration for maximum output on two shafts.

Of about 34 Krivaks built, probably only ten remain operational at the time of writing. At least four were late new-builds for Border Guard service. Known as Krivak IIIs, these have a single 100mm gun forward and helicopter facilities aft.

ABOVE: **A Krivak I identifiable by her 76mm gun mountings aft. She has no helicopter, relying on the VDS (located in the low housing right aft) and bow sonar to provide long-range targeting data for the SS-N-14 ("Silex") AS missiles in the launchers forward.**
LEFT: **In what appears to be a joint Baltic exercise, a German Bremen-class frigate lays astern of a Krivak I. SA-N-4 SAM launchers are housed forward and aft, the directors for each being visible. The SS-N-14 also has an anti-ship capability.**

Krivak II, as built

Displacement: 3,075 tons (standard); 3,500 tons (full load)
Length: 113m/370ft 11in (wl); 123.1m/403ft 7in (oa)
Beam: 13.2m/43ft 3in
Draught: 4.6m/15ft 1in
Armament: 2 x 100mm guns (2x1); 1 xquadruple SS-N-14 SSM launcher; 2 x twin SA-N-4 SAM launchers; 8 x 533m torpedo tubes (2x4); 2 x MBU-6000 AS rocket launchers
Machinery: 2 boost gas turbines, 2 cruise gas turbines, 2 shafts
Power: 2 x 14,920kW/20,000shp and 2 x 5,595kW/7,500shp maximum; 41,030kW/55,000shp for 30.5 knots
Endurance: 7,220kW/3,900nm at 20 knots
Protection: Nominal
Complement: 210

LEFT: **The radar-signature reduction features of** *Stereogushchiy* **combine to make her appear larger than her true size. Note how the masting arrangements on the ship vary from those on the official model (below).**

Steregushchiy class

Following the collapse of the Soviet Union, cuts in defence funding saw the apparent abandonment of several interesting warship classes. These included a helicopter-equipped Krivak replacement in the 3,200-ton Neustrashimyy type, of which only two appear to have been completed, and the 1,600-ton Gepard-class "utility frigate", a concept reminiscent of the British Type 14s and also curtailed at two units.

Looking rather more hopeful, with plans for 10, even 25, ships is the slightly larger Steregushchiy type, which appears to have been aimed at the export market. About 250 tons greater than a Gepard, it can operate a helicopter of the size of a Kamov Ka-27 (Helix A), for which a permanent hangar is provided.

The hull is of the long forecastle type, the low afterdeck being occupied largely by an enclosed VDS, which is roofed over to full hull width by the helipad. The VDS is complemented by a large, low-frequency sonar at the forefoot (of a size

that could cause headaches when stemming the vessel in a small dry dock).

Backing up the helicopter for AS operations, the ship carries two twin heavyweight torpedo tubes, reportedly able to launch the Type 84R Vodopad-NK anti-submarine missile as well as wire-guided torpedoes.

The earlier planned large funnel has been reduced to a stump. A single, dual-purpose 100mm gun is mounted forward. Between it and the bridge front is a low casing which can accommodate a VLS for eight SS-N-25 ("Switchblade") SSMs or a gun/missile CIWS.

Unobtrusively recessed into the deck adjacent to the hangar are silo-housed SA-N-11 ("Grison") close-in anti-aircraft missiles, apparently optional, while flanking the after superstructure are two six-barrelled 30mm Gatling-type weapons.

ABOVE: **Virtually complete, the** *Steregushchiy* **presents a workmanlike appearance. Note the Kortik-M CIWS fitted abaft the gun in place of the reported VLS. This may indicate an export version.**

Armament and electronics fits appear to be flexible, while models indicate optional redesigned upperworks for signature reduction.

Steregushchiy class

Displacement: 1,850 tons (standard); 2,100 tons (full load)
Length: 111.6m/365ft 10in (oa)
Beam: 14m/45ft 10in
Draught: 3.7m/12ft 2in
Armament: 1 x 100mm gun; 2 x 30mm Gatling guns; 8 x SS-N-25 SSM; 64 x SA-N-11 CIWS SAM; 4 x 533mm torpedo tubes (4x1)
Machinery: 4 diesel engines, 2 shafts
Power: 24,767kW/33,200bhp for 26 knots
Endurance: 6,667km/3,600nm at 15 knots
Protection: Not known
Complement: 100

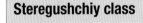

LEFT: **Although there are minor differences, the appearance of the official model is true to that of the ship herself. The very deep fairing around the bow sonar results in deep submergence and a reduced liability to damaging slamming.**

LEFT: **Like their Italian counterparts, German designers preferred a flush-decked small frigate with accommodation gained by a full-width, non-structural deckhouse. Amidships, *Augsburg* is dominated by gas turbine requirements, with outsize funnel and casings.**

Köln class

Products of the same yard as the Hamburg-class destroyers, the six Köln were, in basic respects, diminutives of them. They were the first domestically built fast escorts permitted after 1945, and their designers naturally drew on their earlier experience, both types featuring bow sections remarkably similar to those of post-1943 torpedo boats and destroyers – sharply flared and knuckled, with anchors stowed high up at the deck edge to reduce impact and spray formation.

The Kölns were contemporary with the British Type 81s ("Tribal") and, like them, incorporated the still-new technology of gas-turbine propulsion. Of lower power, the single-screwed British ships cruised on steam, using the gas turbine (which

represented only 37.5 per cent of installed power) in COSAG combination only for high-speed boost and getting under weigh from cold. The Germans installed a CODAG arrangement, coupling a pair of diesel engines and a gas turbine, singly or in combination, to either shaft. The gas turbines here generated some 68 per cent of maximum combined power. The four diesels resulted in somewhat complex gearing arrangements for either shaft but probably were the best available choice from a still-recovering heavy manufacturing industry.

The Kölns' hull was flush-decked, with full-width deckhouse, a form that was repeated with reduced crew on the Hamburgs. A French-sourced single

100mm dual-purpose gun was located at either end, the forward mounting superfired by two quadruple Bofors AS rocket launchers, sited immediately forward of the bridge.

Although fast, bettering 30 knots in service, the Kölns were cramped and had no scope for the addition of a helicopter. With the new Bremen-class frigates entering service from 1982 (confusingly with some repeated names) the Kölns began to be retired. *Karlsruhe* and *Emden* were acquired by Turkey; *Augsburg* and *Lübeck* served into the 1990s. The MEKO frigates that superseded them began an entirely new trend.

LEFT: **Portland, Dorset, where *Lübeck* is seen pierside in company with a British Hecla-class survey ship, a gun-armed Leander and a distant Type 42. Portland long served as a working-up base for newly commissioned European-NATO warships.**

Köln class, as built

Displacement: 2,150 tons (standard); 2,620 tons (full load)
Length: 105m/344ft 3in (bp); 109.9m/360ft 4in (oa)
Beam: 10.8m/35ft 5in
Draught: 3.6m/11ft 6in
Armament: 2 x 100mm guns (2x1); 2 x 4-barrelled 375mm AS rocket launchers; 4 x 533mm torpedo tubes (4x1)
Machinery: 2 gas turbines, 4 diesels, 2 shafts
Power: 2 x 9,698kW/13,000bhp and 4 x 2,238kW/3,000bhp; maximum in CODAG combination; 28,348kW/38,000shp for 30 knots
Endurance: 330 tons fuel for 5,370km/2,900mm at 22 knots
Protection: Nominal
Complement: 210

Thetis class

German waters are notable for their shallowness, limiting the size of ships intended to operate specifically within them. This is particularly true of the Baltic, something of a maritime backwater except that during the early 1960s, the Cold War was at its height. For the not-inconsiderable Soviet naval force based on Leningrad/Kronstadt, the Baltic exits represented the only route to the open sea, and control of the Belts separating the Danish islands could expect to be contested. Considerable numbers of German wooden-hulled minesweepers were under construction (these shallow waters being ideal for mining) but further, offensively armed, units were required to dispute the passage of hostile surface ships and submarines, and for the escort of friendly traffic. Surface-to-surface missiles (once available) and torpedoes were weapons of choice to counter the former, and would eventually be deployed on large numbers of steel- and later composite-hulled fast patrol boats. These, however, were still in the future when the Thetis class was built to address the shallow-water anti-submarine requirement.

As was usual at the time, all five were contracted with a single yard. Again, the design featured the flush-decked hull, full-width deck house and knuckled forward sections that were common to most types of German warships of the period. The flat bridge front was extended in some to provide additional space for the operations room.

No medium-calibre gun was carried. The foredeck was occupied by a quadruple Bofors AS rocket launcher. Four single, heavyweight torpedo tubes were sided abaft the main superstructure, while either depth charges or mines could be accommodated aft. Defensive armament was limited to a twin 40mm mounting, located aft with its control system.

Useful as multi-purpose ships in peacetime, the Thetis class served through to the 1990s.

Thetis class

Displacement: 575 tons (standard); 660 tons (full load)
Length: 65.5m/214ft 9in (bp); 69.8m/228ft 10in (oa)
Beam: 8.2m/26ft 22in
Draught: 2.7m/8ft 10in
Armament: 2 x 40mm guns (1x2); 1 x Bofors 375mm quadruple AS rocket launcher; 4 x 533mm torpedo tubes (4x1)
Machinery: 2 diesel engines, 2 shafts
Power: 5,073kW/6,800bhp for 23.5 knots
Endurance: 78 tons oil for 5,090km/2,750nm at 15 knots
Protection: Nominal
Complement: 48

ABOVE: **Rather late in her career, *Triton* has been renumbered for patrol craft duties. She retains the twin 40mm mountings in the elevated aft position, but has landed her torpedo tubes. Note the broad, flat hull form.**

Bremen class

Known officially as Type 122s when built, but Type 122As since modernization, the Bremen resulted from a co-operative venture with the Dutch, the latter building the Kortenaer in parallel. While there are external similarities, the Bremens differ in their masting, notably with the lofty "Eiffel Tower" construction in place of the Kortenaers' rather bare pole mainmast. Dutch ancestry is evident also in the flush-decked hull, with its long, double-curvature sheer, where succeeding German design favours a raised forecastle, having adequate freeboard with little or no sheer.

LEFT: **Except for their masting, the Bremens closely resemble the Dutch Kortenaers, built as a cooperative venture. Unlike earlier classes, the Type 122/Bremens stemmed from five different yards. This photograph is of the nameship.**

The Bremens are of orthodox layout, with distinct gaps between the three (i.e. bridge, funnel-mainmast and hangar) superstructure blocks. Forward of the bridge is a single OTO-Melara 76mm gun, superfired by the rectangular NATO Sea Sparrow SAM launcher. Prominent atop the bridge are the WM-25 and optical/infra-red fire control system. Immediately abaft the bridge block, two quadruple Harpoon SSM launchers are aligned athwartships.

Where the Kortenaer are all-gas-turbine propelled, the Bremen cruise on diesel engines. The Dutch have Rolls-Royce gas turbines, the Germans Fiat-built American LM 2500s.

Together with a full updating of electronics, the 1990s modernizations saw two fast-reaction RAM (Rolling Airframe Missile) point-defence launchers added to the corners of the hangar roof, the space shared with the low structure supporting the air-search radar antenna. Conspicuous, the full-width hangar is configured for a pair of Super Lynx helicopters. Their airborne "dunking" sonars are complemented by a large,

ABOVE: **A later addition to *Lübeck*'s armament was the two 21-cell RAM launchers prominent atop the hangar. The slightly longer-ranged Sea Sparrow is seen forward, and one of two quadruple Harpoon launchers abaft the bridge structure.**

low-frequency unit at the ships' forefoot. There is also, reportedly, a mine-detecting sonar capability.

To the helicopters' AS torpedoes can be added those from four, fixed 324mm tubes aboard the ships.

No further modernization being considered practical, the Bremens will be retired from 2010.

Type 122A

Displacement: 2,950 tons (standard); 3,800 tons (full load)
Length: 121.8m/399ft 4in (wl); 130m/426ft 3in (oa)
Beam: 14.4m/47ft 3in
Draught: 4.3m/14ft 1in
Armament: 1 x 76mm gun; 8 x Harpoon SSM launchers (2x4); 1 x 8-cell launcher for Sea Sparrow SAM; 2 x 21-round RAM launchers; 4 x 324mm AS torpedo tubes
Machinery: 2 gas turbines, 2 diesels, 2 shafts
Power: 38,046kW/51,000shp or 8,206kW/11,000bhp for 30 knots
Endurance: 610 tons fuel for 10,555km/5,700nm at 17 knots
Protection: Nominal
Complement: 200

LEFT: *Schleswig-Holstein* (left) makes an interesting contrast with the rather smaller Spanish Knox-class *Estremadura* (centre) and the Turkish Perry-class *Gökçeada* (right). The German's powerful shoulders and high freeboard are evident. ABOVE: *Brandenburg* shows her speed. Note how Sea Sparrow is now accommodated in a VLS forward, abaft the RAM launcher which superfires the gun.

Brandenburg class

The four Brandenburgs were designed in accordance with the MEKO principles developed by Blohm and Voss, whose yard led the construction consortium. MEKO (MEhrzweck KOmbination or, roughly, multi-purpose) see as many armament and electronics systems as possible modularized into discrete blocks which can, literally, be dropped into a ship's pre-wired system, being added or removed as required. Ships are thus delivered "for", but not necessarily "with", and can be, in theory at least, outfitted for specific missions.

An obvious drawback is that, with so much of the structure removable, the remaining hull requires to be rather more capacious, and compensated to maintain structural strength. Not surprisingly, therefore, the Brandenburgs, with much the same specification as the preceding Bremens, are of about 25 per cent greater displacement, and are proportionately more beamy to compensate for greater topweight and future growth.

The overall result is a ship which is not only structurally strong but, with its considerable depth, looks it. Freeboard is such that sheer is not required and, as a "stealth" measure, the hull has two gentle knuckles running along the greater part of the length.

The foredeck 76mm gun is superfired by one of the two RAM launchers. Between this and the bridge is a VLS with 16 Sea Sparrow SAM cells. Space is reserved to double this number.

Between the bridge block and the divided uptakes of the CODOG propulsion system are, surprisingly, four MM38 Exocet SSM launchers. A second RAM launcher is located atop the hangar roof, while two fixed AS torpedo tubes fire obliquely through apertures on either side of the hull at upper deck level. There are two Super Lynx helicopters.

Officially termed Type 123s, the Brandenburg are all named after German provinces, or *Länder*, with town/city names now apparently being reserved for smaller vessels such as corvettes.

LEFT: *Brandenburg's* hull, built to MEKO principles, maintains its high freeboard over the greater part of its length, contrasting with the more traditional form of the Bremens (opposite). Note the torpedo tube aperture amidships.

Brandenburg class

Displacement: 3,600 tons (standard); 4,490 tons (full load)

Length: 126.9m/416ft 1in (bp); 138.9m/455ft 4in (oa)

Beam: 15.7m/51ft 6in

Draught: 4.4m/14ft 5in

Armament: 1 x 76mm gun; 4 x Exocet SSM launchers (4x1); 1 x VLS launcher for Sea Sparrow SAM; 2 x 21-round RAM launchers; 4 x 324mm AS torpedo tubes (2x2)

Machinery: 2 gas turbines, 2 diesels, 2 shafts

Power: 38,046kW/51,000shp or 8,206kW/11,000bhp 29.5 knots

Endurance: Over 7,410km/4,000nm at 18 knots

Protection: Nominal

Complement: 219

Sachsen class

Slightly larger than the Brandenburgs, the Type 124, or Sachsen, class share maximum commonality. Enclosed space has been gained by extending both bridge block and hangar to the deck edge. These now complement the subtly angled planes of the shell plating to give a very low radar return. To this end, the apertures for boats, torpedo tubes and accommodation ladders can be blanked off. The process is continued with the carefully configured "masts" supporting the advanced electronics which, for the first time, include three-dimensional, phased-array target designation and tracking radar with four-quadrant fixed antennas.

Although a 155mm modularized gun has been trial-fitted, a 76mm weapon is currently carried forward. Abaft it is the forward RAM mounting and a VLS with a mixed load-out of 24 Standard SM-2 and 32 Sea Sparrow SAMs. Amidships, the Sachsens have reverted to eight Harpoon SSMs. AS torpedo tubes have been tripled and are above deck.

Two Super Lynxes are currently carried, but the hangar is dimensioned to accept the larger NH-90 helicopter flown by the French and Italians.

The machinery layout has been considerably revised to a CODAG configuration, with two diesel engines but only one gas turbine. The diesels now account for about 30 per cent of total power and are used to supplement the gas turbine at maximum speed as well as for cruising.

Active fin stabilizers were fitted in the Brandenburgs, but the Sachsens use actively controlled rudders for the purpose. This is likely to lead to increased wear of steering mechanism and rudder bearings.

ABOVE LEFT: **The sculpted form of the tower bearing the four faces of the APAR radar immediately identify a Sachsen, or Type 124, frigate. Unusually, the faces are orientated along the main axes rather than at 45 degrees.** ABOVE: **On diesels alone, the Sachsens can maintain 18 knots. The machinery configuration is CODAG, i.e. combined diesel and gas turbine. With the latter on-line in combination, 29 knots can be exceeded.**

Probably another "first" for the Sachsens is the provision of dedicated accommodation for female crew members, a measure which, taken to its logical conclusion, will be a major contributor to the increase of warship size and, inevitably, expense.

German frigates work in four-ship squadrons but the fourth Sachsen (*Thüringen*) is yet to be ordered.

LEFT: **In peacetime, port visits, naval occasions and generally "showing the flag" occupy a considerable part of a warship's schedule, and here *Hessen* is dressing overall. The light clearly shows the subtle planes of the hull plating.**

Sachsen class

Displacement: 4,500 tons (standard); 5,690 tons (full load)
Length: 132.2m/433ft 3in (wl); 143m/468ft 10in (oa)
Beam: 16.7m/54ft 9in
Draught: 5m/16ft 4in
Armament: 1 x 76mm gun; 8 x Harpoon SSMs (2x4); 1 x VLS launcher for Standarad SM-2 and Sea Sparrow SAMs; 2 x 21-round RAM launchers; 6 x 324mm AS torpedo tubes (2x3)
Machinery: 1 gas turbine, 2 diesels, 2 shafts
Power: 23,500kW/31,500shp and 15,000kW/20,100bhp for 29.5 knots
Endurance: Over 7,360km/4,000nm at 18 knots
Protection: Nominal
Complement: 242

LEFT: **The diesel-propelled *Braunschweig* has dispensed with a funnel, always a potential target for an IR seeker. Exhaust in early trials, however, has blackened the hull, resulting in a panel being painted black, as seen on the right.**
BELOW: **The class has adopted the Pool-type high holding power anchor. Although lighter, it is stowed low down and is not pocketed. Even in a calm sea, as shown here, it is the cause of spray formation. This, again, is *Braunschweig*.**

Braunschweig class

Now firmly established as both a European and a NATO power, a united Germany is increasing its profile at a global level, her navy consequently undertaking more foreign deployments. Its large, capable, and very expensive frigates are its new capital ships, and there is room for smaller and simpler general-purpose vessels. The considerable flotillas of missile-armed fast patrol boats, built primarily to contest the Baltic exits have, with the relaxation of East–West tensions, lost much of their major role. The newest is also 25 years of age, old for a minor warship. Their replacements, not surprisingly, are light frigates/corvettes of considerably greater size and capability, a consequence of which has already been the reduction of the programme from a planned 15 units to just 5.

The early design favoured the flexibility of the MEKO concept but, on so small a scale, the weight penalty was excessive. The Braunschweig, or Type 130, hull is of long forecastle type, the low afterdeck forming a helipad large enough to handle a Lynx or NH-90, but with only basic facilities. Hangar space is provided only for two drone helicopters, used primarily in surveillance.

Seemingly unsettled in their choice of SSM, the Germans, having already deployed Exocet and Harpoon on their frigates, have specified the 100km/62-mile Saab RBS-15 for the Braunschweigs. Dynamically programmable, this weapon is virtually a cruise missile, and can be used in land attack against designated targets.

A 76mm gun and a pair of RAM launchers are common with larger ships, but, for propulsion, the Type 130s are all-diesel, with one engine on either shaft. There is no funnel, exhaust gases being sea water-cooled to reduce IR signature.

The data stream from the drone helicopters is fused with that from the shipboard electronics systems for target designation and guidance.

ABOVE: ***Erfurt* is seen here fitting out alongside at her Emden builders. Although classed as corvettes, ships of this class are very capable. They can deploy a Lynx-sized helicopter but can hangar only two small drone machines.**

Braunschweig class

Displacement: 1,690 tons (full load)
Length: 82.8m/271ft 6in (bp); 88.8m/290ft 11in (oa)
Beam: Not known
Draught: Not known
Armament: 1 x 76mm gun; 4/12 x Saab RBS-15 SSMs; 2 x 21-round RAM launchers
Machinery: 2 diesel engines, 2 shafts
Power: 14,920kW/20,000bhp for 26.5 knots
Endurance: Over 7,410km/4,000nm at 15 knots
Protection: Nominal
Complement: 65

Van Heemskerck/Kortenaer class

As already noted, the Kortenaer had a common ancestry with the German Bremens but differed visually, particularly in having a pole mainmast and a solid pyramid supporting the fire control radar atop the bridge. Both classes had gas turbine main machinery, but where the Bremens cruised on diesels, the Kortenaers used Tyne gas turbines, with the machinery arranged COGOG fashion.

The Dutch do not use the RAM point-defence system favoured by the Germans. Complementing the Sea Sparrow launcher in "B" position, the earlier Kortenaers had a second 76mm gun on the hangar roof. Later ships had light automatic weapons until Goalkeeper 30mm CIWS was acquired and fitted throughout the class. Eight Harpoon SSMs were located immediately abaft the bridge and four lightweight AS torpedo tubes could be shipped when required.

Two Lynx-sized helicopters could be accommodated in the full-width hangar, upon whose roof was located the conspicuous antenna of the long range air search radar.

Two of the ten Kortenaers were sold new to Greece in 1981 and were replaced by *Jacob van Heemskerck* and *Witte de With*, completed to a modified specification as guided-missile frigates, commissioning several years after the remainder of their near-sisters.

The van Heemskercks sacrificed their AS air component for a Standard SM-1 area defence SAM system, whose launcher is located atop the long, low superstructure that replaced the hangar. No 76mm gun is carried, while the Goalkeeper has been relocated right aft. In contrast with the standard Kortenaers, the stern is fully plated-in.

Between 1993 and 2002, the remaining eight Kortenaers were also acquired by Greece and a current rolling

ABOVE LEFT: **The Kortenaers were of compact but pleasing appearance, dominated aft by a large, near full-width hangar, upon whose roof *Abraham Crijnssen* has a Goalkeeper CIWS. Harpoon is just visible forward of the funnel.** ABOVE: **Two Kortenaers were completed as Guided Missile Frigates. The Standard SM-1 MR magazine and launcher have here replaced the helicopter hangar and flight pad on *Witte de With*. She lacks a 76mm gun forward but has CIWS aft.**

modernization programme seeks to extent their lives by 15 years. It was speculated that the two Heemskercks, retired early, would follow the remainder of the class, but they were acquired by Chile complete with Standard.

LEFT: *Jacob van Heemskerck* has a more complex electronics fit than a standard Kortenaer. The larger dishes forward and aft are for Standard SM-1 control, while the smaller dish on the "foremast" gives guidance for the adjacent Sea Sparrow.

Kortenaer class, final specification

Displacement: 3,000 tons (standard); 3,785 tons (full load)
Length: 121.8m/399ft 4in (bp); 130.2m/426ft 10in (oa)
Beam: 14.4m/47ft 3in
Draught: 4.4m/14ft 5in
Armament: 1 x 76mm gun; 8 x Harpoon SSM launchers (2x4); 1 x 8-cell Sea Sparrow SAM launcher; 4 x 324mm AS torpedo tubes (2x2)
Machinery: 2 Olympus gas turbines, 2 Tyne cruise gas turbines, 2 shafts
Power: 38,494kW/51,600shp for 30 knots or 7,311kW/9,800shp for 20 knots
Endurance: 8,705km/4,700nm at 16 knots
Protection: Nominal
Complement: 200

De Zeven Provinciën class

The gradual transfer of Kortenaers to Greece was offset by the construction of the six Karel Doorman general-purpose frigates and four larger Zeven Provinciëns, described as Air Defence and Command Frigates. The latter were to have been another co-operative project with Germany, in this case joined by Spain. The latter partner withdrew, although the resulting four Alvaro de Bazan class obviously owe much to work already done, but are heavily influenced by American Aegis technology. Germany then pulled out, her four Sachsens being based on preferred MEKO principles. Where both classes have a recognizable common ancestry with the Dutch ships, the latter reflect current French practice.

The Zeven Provinciëns are of long forecastle design, but this is not immediately apparent as the extremities are linked by a continuous knuckle, whose elegant curve divides the slight outward flare of the hull plating from the inwardly inclined, and virtually unbroken, sides of the superstructure blocks. These signature-reducing measures are continued in every "vertical" surface, and particularly in the towers incorporating the APAR phased-array radar and SMART-L early warning radar, both products of Dutch technology.

Somewhat hindered in depression by an inclined forward bulwark, the gun has been upgraded to a 127mm OTO-Melara weapon, abaft which are the flush-fitting covers of a 40-cell Vertical Launch System (VLS), designed for mixed load-outs of Standard SM-2 and Improved Sea Sparrow SAMs.

Equally unobtrusive are the eight Harpoon SSMs, concealed amidships behind inclined panels. One Goalkeeper CIWS is located over the bridge, another aft on the hangar roof.

Paired AS torpedo tubes fire through small apertures in the shell plating immediately forward of the hangar,

LEFT: **The distinctive faceted tower housing the APAR three-dimensional, phased-array, target designation and tracking radar dominates *Tromp*'s profile. Abaft the 127mm gun she is fitted with a 40-cell VLS.**

ABOVE LEFT: **Frigate designers are currently suffering from a bad attack of "radar invisibility", resulting in ships of closely similar appearance. Although a trifle bland, *de Zeven Provinciën*'s sharply sculpted form is still quite pleasing.** ABOVE: **A study in shapes: in the foreground, the elegant lines of the US Aegis cruiser *Normandy* framing the Dutch *Evertsen*, and beyond, a Danish Niels Juel corvette. The inclined black rectangle of *Evertsen*'s SMART-L radar also appears on British Darings.**

which is dimensioned to accommodate a single NH-90 helicopter.

Propulsion is of CODAG configuration, the ships cruising on diesels but using a pair of Spey gas turbines for high speed.

De Zeven Provinciën class

Displacement: 5,870 tons (standard); 6,050 tons (full load)
Length: 130.2m/426ft 11in (bp); 144.2m/472ft 11in (oa)
Beam: 17.2m/56ft 4in
Draught: 5.2m/17ft 1in
Armament: 1 x 127mm gun; 8 x Harpoon SSM launchers (2x4); 1 x 40-cell VLS for Standard SM-2 and Improved Sea Sparrow SAMs; 2 x 30mm Goalkeeper CIWS; 4 x 324mm AS torpedo tubes (2x2)
Machinery: 2 gas turbines, 2 diesels, 2 shafts
Power: 39,000kW/52,280shp for 30 knots or 8,400kW/11,260bhp for 19 knots
Endurance: 9,260km/5,000nm at 18 knots
Protection: Nominal
Complement: 202

Karel Doorman class

Representing the "Lo" end of the "Hi-Lo" frigate force were the eight so-called "M"-class ships, effectively scaled-down Kortenaers. In service, they adopted the name of the lead ship. As in the UK, government policy is to reduce naval strength while having to recognize that the rump of a great shipbuilding industry no longer has work sufficient to justify its existence. The Ms, therefore, were ordered ahead of schedule, which served only to accelerate the disposal of the Kortenaers in compensation. At the time of writing, the Ms – the latest just 13 years in service – are themselves slated for transfer abroad.

Pre-dating the more capable de Zeven Provinciën class by some years, the Doormans lack the extreme profiling adopted to reduce radar and IR signatures. The hull has a gentle knuckle, running the greater part of its length, but the superstructure, despite its "vertical" surfaces being slightly inclined, remains conventional in layout.

The solidly plated mast is unusually tall, and is flanked by two prominent radomes for SATCOM antennas. There is a 76mm gun forward and, abaft the funnel, space for two quadruple Harpoon SSMs, rarely carried. Within the after superstructure are two pairs of lightweight AS torpedo tubes.

The hangar is dimensioned for only one Lynx-sized helicopter as it is flanked by eight Sea Sparrow launcher cells on either side. There is no capacity for Standard SM-2 missiles. This after superstructure is dominant, bearing on its roof the large standard antenna of the Dutch-built LW-08 early warning radar and, on its starboard after corner, a single Goalkeeper CIWS, again not always fitted. Later units can deploy towed array passive sonars.

Currently, two of the class are to be transferred to each of Belgium, Chile and Portugal. The remaining pair will undoubtedly follow.

ABOVE: **Originally termed M-class frigates, the Karel Doormans have an unusual Sea Sparrow SAM arrangement, 16 missiles being located in pairs on the port side of the hangar. *Van Amstel* has hers partly concealed by a radar-reflecting panel.**

LEFT: **Only 12 years of age, *Abraham van der Hulst* was one of two M-class ships sold to Chile in 2004. Unchanged except for modified helicopter arrangements, she is seen here en route to a new career in South America as the *Almirante Blanco Encalada*.**

Karel Doorman class

Displacement: 2,800 tons (standard); 3,320 tons (full load)
Length: 114.4m/375ft 1in (bp); 122.2m/400ft 9in (oa)
Beam: 13.1m/43ft
Draught: 4.3m/14ft 1in
Armament: 1 x 76mm gun; 8 x Harpoon SSM launchers (2x4); 2 x 8-cell VLS launchers for Improved Sea Sparrow SAM; 1 x 30mm Goalkeeper CIWS; 4 x 324mm AS torpedo tubes (2x2)
Machinery: 2 gas turbines, 2 diesels, 2 shafts
Power: 36,000kW/48,257shp for 29 knots or 6,300kW/8,450bhp for 21 knots
Endurance: Over 9,260km/5,000nm at 18 knots
Protection: Nominal
Complement: 154

St. Laurent class

This extended class of 20 frigates replaced the last of the war-built anti-submarine force. Their enclosed design emphasized operations in hostile northern waters and low temperatures. The hull was flush-decked and of high freeboard, the after end encompassing a long, open well containing two Limbo mortars and, with later modernization, a VDS. Except in way of the full-width deckhouse under the bridge, the sheerstrake was radiused over the entire length of the ship. Most of the anchor gear was located below the forecastle deck, clear of ice formation. The anchors themselves were recessed into pockets, with covers to reduce spray formation and further ice accretion. As this can add

dangerously to topweight, this may have influenced the decision to construct the superstructure mainly in aluminium alloy.

As designed, the ships mounted two 3in 50 mountings, but the after one was landed during later modifications. The forward mounting was situated on a low, raised platform, behind a breakwater.

The extended timescale, with construction shared between six yards, saw modifications introduced to the extent that few ships were alike, and these quickly changed with further updates during their long careers.

In the original Limbo-armed version there was a single, tapered funnel and a short, plated-in mast with lattice extensions. Some later landed one

ABOVE LEFT: *Fraser* shows something of the St. Laurents' magnificent seakeeping qualities in a short Atlantic swell. Her 3in gun mounting is trained aft to minimize water ingress. She was remodelled in the early 1980s to operate a large AS helicopter. ABOVE: *Terra Nova* of the Restigouche group has retained much of her original configuration, but with an ASROC (not visible here) replacing one of her Limbo mortars. Note the unusually lofty mast and the anchor pocket shuttered to reduce spray formation.

Limbo, along with the after gun mounting, in order to accommodate an 8-cell ASROC launcher amidships. Half the class lost both Limbos, the well being covered with an elevated flight pad for a single Sea King helicopter. The provision of its amidships hangar required the uptakes to be split, with a separate casing on either side. To the helicopter's "dunking" sonar and AS torpedoes, the ship added VDS and six AS torpedo tubes.

The ships proved to be remarkably durable, most serving into the 1990s.

St. Laurent class, as designed

Displacement: 2,260 tons (standard); 2,800 tons (full load)
Length: 111.6m/366ft (oa)
Beam: 12.8m/42ft
Draught: 4m/13ft 3in
Armament: 4 x 3in guns (2x2); 2 x Limbo 3-barrelled AS mortars
Machinery: Geared steam turbines, 2 boilers, 2 shafts
Power: 22,380kW/30,000shp for 28.5 knots
Endurance: 8,800km/4,750nm at 14 knots
Protection: None
Complement: 230

ABOVE: Following her 1980s DELEX modernization, *Restigouche* has acquired a reloadable ASROC installation. Most of her Limbo well has been plated-over, but her stern has been modified to accept a large American VDS. During their long careers, the ships acquired many individual characteristics.

LEFT: **Very considerably modernized during the early 1990s, the Iroquois class emerged as capable ships.** *Algonquin*'s VLS, **visible forward of the 76mm gun, is configured for Standard SM-2 SAMs. CIWS is atop the hangar and AS torpedo tubes are abreast the flight pad.**
BELOW: **The Halifax class is fitted with a Bofors 57mm gun forward. Visible abreast of the funnel of** *Charlottetown* **is the port side, vertical-launch Sea Sparrow installation, obscuring the Harpoon launchers.**

Iroquois and Halifax classes

Carrying some of the "Tribal" names made famous during World War II, the four Iroquois of the early 1970s introduced gas turbine propulsion to the Royal Canadian Navy. Considerably larger than the St. Laurents, more heavily armed and with some command facilities, they were classed as destroyers, although still primarily AS vessels.

Their dimensions were driven by the then-bold decision to accommodate two large, Sea King-sized helicopters. Hulls were sufficiently spacious to install a passive anti-rolling system, effective at low speeds when there is inadequate flow over active stabilizing fins.

During the 1990s they were considerably updated. In place of the 5in gun appeared a recessed VLS, accommodating 29 Standard SM-2 SAMs, superfired by a 76mm OTO-Melara weapon. Cruising gas turbines were upgraded and the split exhaust casings replaced by a single large funnel. A Vulcan Phalanx CIWS was installed atop the hangar and a VDS aft.

Meanwhile, the 12-strong Halifax class was built to replace the aging St. Laurents. Despite their "frigate" label, they carry only one helicopter but are as large, and virtually as fast, as the Iroquois. They also carry Harpoon SSMs and, given small differences in layout, are comparable with the Royal Navy's Type 23s.

For improved physical protection, the Harpoons are located immediately forward of the hangar, while the VLS for the Sea Sparrow SAMs is a split, above-deck installation, flanking the enormous funnel, screened by a reflective panel.

The main propulsion units have been changed from the Iroquois' Pratt & Whitneys to the more widely used General Electric LM-2500 while, in CODOG configuration, a medium-speed diesel is used for cruising. Despite budget cuts, the class is due for thorough upgrading, including the addition of a Dutch-sourced three-dimensional search radar and an active/passive towed array sonar.

Halifax class, as built

Displacement: 4,300 tons (standard); 4,760 tons (full load)
Length: 124.5m/408ft 2in (bp); 135.5m/444ft 3in (oa)
Beam: 14.8m/48ft 6in
Draught: 4.9m/16ft 1in
Armament: 1 x 57mm gun; 8 x Harpoon SSM launchers (2x4); 2 x 8-cell VLS for Sea Sparrow SAM; 1 x Vulcan Phalanx CIWS; 4 x 324mm AS torpedo tubes (2x2)
Machinery: 2 gas turbines, 1 diesel, 2 shafts
Power: 35,435kW/47,500shp for 29 plus knots or 6,472kW/8,675shp for 18 knots
Endurance: 550 tons fuel for 8,335km/4,500nm at 20 knots
Protection: Nominal
Complement: 224

LEFT: **Nameship of an eight-strong class, *Anzac* is seen off a Gulf oil terminal, her MEKO 200 origin clearly recognizable. She is fitted with two quadruple Harpoon SSM forward and abaft the funnels, a VLS for Sea Sparrow.** ABOVE: ***Anzac* again, this time leaving Portsmouth, England, without Harpoon and the Vulcan Phalanx CIWS on the hangar roof. Electronics are a Franco-British/German/Swedish/American mix.**

Anzac class

Previously dependent upon British and American designs, Australia and New Zealand turned to Germany for the Anzacs. These were intended to replace both Adams-class destroyers and River-class (i.e. modified Type 12/Leander) frigates, two very different types of ship. Their role could be high-risk as part of a multinational force, or low-risk in policing very long coastlines and large areas of ocean. Although Australia currently faces no obvious external threat, she is increasingly prepared to shoulder the responsibilities of regional power.

Short-listed for consideration were the German MEKO 200 (of which three had been recently and fortuitously completed for Portugal), the Dutch Karel Doorman and the "Yarrow frigate". The first-named won because of its "for, but not with" design, making it capable of being fitted for specific missions. Australia contracted for eight units, with New Zealand opting for just a pair. All were Australian-built.

On a more limited scale, the Anzacs follow the general MEKO principles featured above in the Germany section. It is worth remembering that a module for,

say, a 5in 54 gun is as large for a 3,300-tonner as it is for a ship of 5,700 tons.

As delivered, the ships for both navies were similarly equipped. Forward is a 5in gun, abaft the split funnel an 8-cell VLS for Sea Sparrow SAMs. For these, space is allocated for a second 8-cell block. Margins are also provided for both eight Harpoon SSMs and a Vulcan Phalanx CIWS. Only the New Zealanders currently carry the latter.

All carry an American Super Sea Sprite LAMPS helicopter but, currently, no AS torpedo tubes. For economy, only one LM-2500 gas turbine is fitted for boost, limiting maximum speed to about 27 knots.

Anzac class, with full planned outfit

Displacement: 3,250 tons (standard); 3,550 tons (full load)
Length: 109.5m/359ft (bp); 117.5m/385ft 3in (oa)
Beam: 13.8m/45ft 3in
Draught: 4.2m/13ft 9in
Armament: 1 x 5in gun; 8 x Harpoon SSMs (2x4); 1 x 8-cell VLS for Imp. Sea Sparrow; 1 x Vulcan Phalanx CIWS; 6 x 324mm AS torpedo tubes (2x3)
Machinery: 1 gas turbine, 2 diesels, 2 shafts
Power: 22,500kW/30,160shp for over 27 knots or 6,600kW/8,847bhp for 20 knots
Endurance: 423 tons fuel for 11,040km/6,000nm at 18 knots
Protection: Nominal
Complement: 148

ABOVE: **Australian-built in the same series were two near-identical Anzacs for New Zealand. This is *Te Kaha*, with NATO-series numbering, in contrast to the Australian's US Navy style.**

Class lists

Page 30 Black Swan class: *Black Swan, Erne, Flamingo, Ibis, Whimbrel, Wild Goose, Woodcock, Woodpecker, Wren.* Modified Black Swan class: *Actaeon, Alacrity, Amethyst, Chanticlear, Crane, Cygnet, Hart, Hind, Kite, Lapwing, Lark, Magpie, Mermaid, Modeste, Nereide, Opossum, Peacock, Pheasant, Redpole, Snipe, Sparrow, Starling.*

Page 31 Hunt class Type I: *Atherstone, Berkeley, Cattistock, Cleveland, Cotswold, Cottesmore, Eglinton, Exmoor, Fernie, Garth, Hambledon, Holderness, Mendip, Meynell, Pytchley, Quantock, Southdown, Tynedale, Whaddon.* Type II: *AvonVale, Badsworth, Beaufort, Bicester, Blackmore, Blankney, Blencathra, Brocklesby, Calpe, Chiddingfold, Cowdray, Croome, Dulverton, Eridge, Farndale, Grove, Heythrop, Hurworth, Lamerton, Lauderdale, Ledbury, Liddesdale, Middleton, Puckeridge, Southwold, Tetcott, Oakley, Wheatland, Wilton, Zetland.* Type III: *Airedale, Albrighton, Aldenham, Belvoir, Blean, Bleasdale, Derwent, Easton, Eggesford, Goathland, Haydon, Holcombe, Limbourne, Melbreak, Penylan, Rockwood, Stevenstone, Talybont, Tanatside, Wensleydale.* Type IV: *Brecon, Brissenden.*

Page 32 Flower class UK-built, 1939 Programme: *Anemone, Arbutus, Asphodel, Aubretia, Auricula, Begonia, Bluebell, Campanula, Candytuft, Carnation, Celandine, Clematis, Columbine, Convolvulus, Coreopsis, Crocus, Cyclamen, Dianella, Dahlia, Delphinium, Dianthus, Gardenia, Geranium, Gladiolus, Godetia, Heliotrope, Hollyhock, Honeysuckle, Hydrangea, Jasmine, Jonquil, Larkspur, Lavender, Lobelia, Marguerite, Marigold, Mignonette, Mimosa, Myosotis, Narcissus, Nigella, Penstemon, Polyanthus, Primrose, Salvia, Snapdragon, Snowdrop, Sunflower, Tulip, Verbena, Veronica, Wallflower, Zinnia.* UK-built, 1939 Emergency Programme: *Acanthus, Aconite, Alyssum, Amaranthus, Arabis, Bellwort, Borage, Burdock, Calendula, Camellia, Campion, Clarkia, Clover, Coriander, Coltsfoot, Erica, Fleur de Lys, Freesia, Gentian, Gloxinia, Heartsease, Heather, Hybiscus, Hyacinth, Kingcup, La Malouine, Loosestrife, Lotus (I), Lotus (II), Mallow, Meadowsweet, Nasturtium, Orchis, Oxlip, Pennywort, Peony, Periwinkle, Petunia, Picotee, Pimpernel, Renunculus, Rhododendron, Rockrose, Rose, Samphire, Saxifrage, Spiraea, Starwort, Stonecrop, Sundew, Violet.*

ABOVE: *Jasmine,* Flower class.

UK-built, 1940 Programme: *Abelia, Alisma, Anchusa, Armeria, Aster, Bergamot, Bryony, Buttercup, Chrysanthemum, Cowslip, Eglantine, Fritillary, Genista, Vervain, Vetch.* Supplementary Programmes: *Arrowhead, Balsam, Bittersweet, Eyebright, Fennel, Godetia, (II), Hepatica, Hyderabad, Mayflower, Monkshood, Montbretia, Pink, Poppy, Potentilla, Quesnell, Snowberry, Sorrel, Spikenard, Sweetbriar, Tamarisk, Thyme, Trillium, Windflower.* UK-built Modified Flower class, 1941–42: *Arabis, Arbutus, Betony, Buddleia, Bugloss, Bulrush, Burnet, Candytuft, Ceanothus, Charlock.* Canadian-built, Flower class, 1939–40 Programme: *Agassiz, Alberni, Algoma, Amherst, Arrowhead, Arvida, Baddeck, Barrie, Battleford, Brandon, Buctouche, Camrose, Chambly, Chicoutimi, Chilliwack, Cobalt, Collingwood, Dauphin, Dawson, Drumheller, Dunvegan, Edmondston, Galt, Kamloops, Kamsack, Kenogami, Lethbridge, Levis, Louisburg, Lunenburg, Matapedia, Moncton, Moosejaw, Morden, Nanaimo, Napanee, Oakville, Orillia, Pikton, Prescott, Quesnel, Rimouski, Rosthern, Sackville, Saskatoon, Shawinigan, Shediac, Sherbrooke, Sorel, Subbury, Summerside, The Pas, Wetaskiwin, Weyburn.* Revised Canadian Flower class 1941–42 Programme: *Calgary, Charlottetown, Dundas, Fredericton, Halifax, La Malbaie, Port Arthur, Regina, Ville de Quebec, Woodstock.* 1942–43 Programme: *Athol, Coburg, Fergus, Frontenac, Guelph, Hawksbury, Lindsay, Norsyd, North Bay, Owen Sound, Rivière du Loup, St. Lambert, Trentonian, Whitby.* 1943–44 Programme: *Asbestos, Beauharnois, Bellville, Lachute, Merrittonia, Parry Sound, Peterborough, Smith's Falls, Stellaton, Strathroy, Thorlock, West, York.* Canadian-built for USN: *Comfrey, Cornel, Flax, Mandrake, Milfoil, Musk, Nepeta, Privet.* Canadian-built to RN via USN: *Dittany, Honesty, Linaria, Rosebay, Smilax, Statice, Willowherb.*

Page 33 River class 1940 Programme: *Balinderry, Bann, Chelmer, Dart, Derg, Ettrick, Exe, Itchen, Jed, Kale, Lagan, Moyola, Ness, Nith, Rother, Spey, Strule, Swale, Tay, Test, Teviot, Trent, Tweed, Waveney, Wear.* 1941 Programme: *Aire, Braid, Cam, Deveron, Dovey, Fal, Frome, Helford, Helmsdale, Meon, Nene, Plym, Ribble, Tavy, Tees, Torridge, Towy, Usk, Windrush, Wye.* 1942 Programme: *Avon, Awe, Halladale, Lochy, Mourne, Nadder, Odzani, Taff.* Canadian-built for RN: *Barle, Cuckmere, Evenlode, Findhorn, Inver, Lossie, Parret, Shiel.* Canadian-built River class 1942–43 Programme: *Beacon Hill, Cap de la Madeleine, Cape Breton, Charlottetown, Chebogue, Dunver, Eastview, Gron, Joliette, Jonquière, Kirkland Lake, Kokanee, La Hulloise, Longuenil, Magog, Matane, Montreal, New Glasgow, New Waterford, Orkney, Outremont, Port Colborne, Prince Rupert, St. Catherines, St. John, Springhill, Stettler, Stormont, Swansea, Thetford*

Mines, Valleyfield, Waskesiu, Wentworth. 1943–44 Programme: *Antigonish, Buckingham, Capilano, Carlplace, Coaticook, Fort Erie, Glace Bay, Hallowell, Inch Arran, Lanark, Lasalle, Levis, Penetang, Poundmaker, Prestonian, Royal Mount, Runnymede, St. Pierre, St. Stephan, Ste. Thérèse, Seacliff, Stonetown, Strathadam, Sussexvale, Toronto, Victoriaville.*

Page 34 Castle class, 1942 Programme: *Allington Castle, Bamborough C., Caistor C., Denbigh C., Farnham C., Hadleigh C., Hedingham C., Hurst C., Kenilworth C., Lancaster C., Oakham C.* 1943 Programme: *Alnwick Castle, Amberley C., Berkeley C., Carisbrooke C., Dumbarton C., Flint C., Knaresborough C., Launceston C., Leeds C., Morpeth C., Oxford C., Pevensey C., Portchester C., Rushen C., Tintagel C.* Transferred to RCN: *Guildford Castle, Hedingham C., Hever C., Norham C., Nunnery C., Pembroke C., Rising C., Sandgate C., Sherborne C., Tamworth C., Walmer C., Wolvesey C.* Transferred to Norway: *Shrewsbury Castle.*

Page 35 Bay class: *Bigbury Bay, Burghead Bay, Cardigan Bay, Carnarvon Bay, Cawsand B., Enard B., Largo Bay, Morecambe B., Mounts B., Padstow B., Porlock B., St. Bride's B., St. Austell B., Start B., Tremadoc B., Veryan B., Whitesand B., Widemouth B., Wigtown Bay.* Loch class, 1942 Programme: *Loch Achanalt, Loch Dunvegan, Loch Eck, Loch Fada.* 1943 Programme: *Loch Achray, L. Alvie, L. Arkaig, L. Craggie, L. Fyne, L. Glendhu, L. Gorm, L. Insh, L. Katrine, L. Killin, L. Killisport, L. Lomond, L. More, L. Morlich, L. Quoich, L. Ruthwen, L. Scavaig, L. Shin, L. Tarbert, L. Tralaig, Loch Veyatie.* Transferred to RCN: *Loch Achanalt, L. Alvie, L. Morlich.* Transferred to South Africa: *Loch Ard, L. Boisdale, L. Cree.*

Page 36 Type 15 conversions: *Rapid, Relentless, Rocket, Roebuck, Troubridge, Grenville, Ulster, Ulysses, Undaunted, Undine, Urania, Urchin, Ursa, Venus, Verulam, Vigilant, Virago, Volage, Wakeful, Whirlwind, Wizard, Zest.* Type 16 conversions: *Orwell, Paladin, Petard, Teazer, Tenacious, Termagent, Terpsichore, Tumult, Tuscan, Tyrian.*

Page 37 Type 14: *Blackwood, Duncan, Dundas, Exmouth, Grafton, Hardy, Keppel, Malcolm, Murray, Palliser, Pellew, Russell.*

Page 38 Type 41: *Jaguar, Leopard, Lynx, Puma.* Type 61: *Chichester, Lincoln, Llandaff, Salisbury.*

Page 39 Type 12: *Berwick, Blackpool, Brighton, Eastbourne, Falmouth, Londonderry, Lowestoft, Plymouth, Rhyl, Rothesay, Torquay, Whitby, Yarmouth.* Leander class: *Ajax, Arethusa, Argonaut, Aurora, Cleopatra, Danae, Euryalus, Galatea, Juno, Leander, Minerva, Naiad, Penelope, Phoebe, Sirius.* Improved Leander class: *Achilles, Andromeda, Apollo, Ariadne, Bacchante, Charybdis, Diomede, Hermione, Jupiter, Scylla.*

Page 40 Type 21: *Active, Alacrity, Amazon, Ambuscade, Antelope, Ardent, Arrow, Avenger.*

Page 41 Type 22: *Battleaxe, Brazen, Brilliant, Broadsword.* Batch II: *Beaver, Boxer, Brave, Coventry, London, Sheffield.* Batch III: *Campbeltown, Chatham, Cornwall, Cumberland.*

ABOVE: ***Balny*, Commandant Rivière class.**

Page 42 Type 23: *Argyll, Grafton, Iron Duke, Kent, Lancaster, Marlborough, Monmouth, Montrose, Norfolk, Northumberland, Portland, Richmond, St. Albans, Somerset, Sutherland, Westminster.*

Page 43 Le Corse class: *Le Bordelais, Le Boulonnais, Le Brestois, Le Corse.* Le Normand class: *L'Agenais, l'Alsacien, Le Basque, Le Béarnais, Le Bourguignon, Le Breton, Le Champenois, Le Gascon, Le Lorrain, Le Normand, Le Picard, Le Provençal, Le Savoyard, Le Vendéen.*

Page 44 Commandant Rivière class: *Amiral Charner, Balny, Commandant Bory, Commandant Bourdais, Commandant Rivière, Doudart de la Grée, Enseigne Henry, Protet, Victor Schoelcher.*

Page 45 *Aconit.*

Page 46 D'Estienne d'Orves class: *Amyot d'Invilles, Commandant Birot, Commandant Blaison, Commandant Bouan, Commandant de Pimodan, Commandant Ducuing, Commandant l'Herminier, D'Estienne d'Orves, Detroyat, Drogou, Enseigne de Vaisseau Jacoubet, Jean Moulin, Lieutenant de Vaisseau Lavallée, Lieutenant de Vaisseau le Henaff, Premier Maître l'Her, Quartier-Maître Anquetil, Second Maître le Bihan.*

Page 47 Floréal class: *Floréal, Germinal, Nivôse, Prairial, Vendémiaire, Ventôse.*

Page 48 La Fayette class: *Aconit, Courbet, Guépratte, La Fayette, Surcouf.*

Page 49 Shumushu class: *Hachijo, Ishigaki, Kunashiri, Shumushu.* Etorofu class: *Amakusa, Etorofu, Fukue, Hirato, Iki, Kanju, Kasado, Manju, Matsuwa, Mutsure, Oki, Sado, Tsushima, Wakamiya.*

Page 50 Mikura class: *Awagi, Chiburi, Kurahashi, Kusagaki, Mikura, Miyake, Nomi, Yashiro.* Ukuru class: *Aguni, Amani, Chikubu, Daito, Habushi, Habuto, Hiburi, Hodaka, Ikara, Ikino, Ikuna, Inagi, Iwo, Kanawa, Kozu, Kuga, Kume, Mokuto, Murotsu, Oga, Okinawa, Otsu, Sakito, Shiga, Shinnan, Shisaka, Shonan, Takane, Tomoshiri, Uku, Ukuru, Urumi, Yaku.*

Page 51 Kaibokan Type I: Odd numbers 1–235. Kaibokan Type II: Even numbers 2–204. Matsu class: *Azusa, Enoki, Hagi Hatsuyume, Hatsuzakura, Hinoki, Hishi, Kaba, Kaede, Kaki, Kashi, Katsura, Kaya, Keyaki, Kiri, Kusunoki, Kuwa, Kuzu, Maki, Matsu, Momi, Momo, Nara, Nashi, Nire, Odake, Sakaki, Sakura, Shi, Sugi, Sumire, Tachibana, Take, Tochi, Tsubaki, Tsuta, Ume, Wakazakura, Yadake, Yaezkura, Yanagi.*

Page 52 Ikazuchi class: *Ikazuchi, Inazuma.* Isuzu class: *Isuzu, Kitakami, Mogami, Oi.*

ABOVE: **McCloy, Bronstein class.**

Page 53 Chikugo class: *Ayase, Chitose, Chikugo, Iwase, Kumano, Mikuma, Niyodo, Noshiro, Teshio, Tokachi, Yoshino.*
Page 54 Ishikari/Yubari class: *Yubari, Yubetsu.*
Page 55 Abukuma class: *Abukuma, Chikuma, Jintsu, Oyodo, Sendai, Tone.*
Page 56–7 Buckley class: *Ahrens, Alexander J. Luke, Amesbury, Barber, Barr, Bates, Blessman, Borum, Bowers, Buckley, Bull, Bunch, Burke, Charles Lawrence, Chase, Cofer, Coolbaugh, Cronin, Currier, Damon M. Cummings, Daniel T. Griffin, Darby, Donnell, Durik, Earl V. Johnson, Eichenberger, England, Enright, Fechteler, Fieberling, Fogg, Foreman, Foss, Fowler, Frament, Francis M. Robinson, Frybarger, Gantner, Gendreau, George, George W. Ingram, Gillette, Greenwood, Gunason, Haines, Harmon, Hayter, Henry R. Kenyon, Hollis, Holton, Hopping, Ira Jeffery, J. Douglas Blackwood, Jack W. Wilke, James E. Craig, Jenks, Jordon, Joseph C. Hubbard, Joseph E. Campbell, Kephart, Laning, Lee Fox, Liddle, Lloyd, Loeser, Lovelace, Loy, Major, Maloy, Manning, Marsh, Neuendorf, Newman, Osmus, Otter, Paul G. Baker, Raby, Reeves, Reuben James, Rich, Robert I. Paine, Runels, Schmitt, Scott, Scroggins, Sims, Solar, Spangenberg, Spangler, Tatum, Thomason, Underhill, Vanmen, Varian, Weber, Weeden, Whitehurst, William C. Cole, William T. Powell, Willmarth, Wiseman, Witter.* Cannon class: *Acree, Alger, Amick, Atherton, Baker, Baugust, Baron, Booth, Bostwick, Breeman, Bright, Bronstein, Burrows, Cannon, Carroll, Carter, Cates, Christopher, Clarence E. Evans, Coffman, Cooner, Curtis W. Howard, Earl K. Olsen, Ebert, Eisner, Eldridge, Gandy, Garfield Thomas, Gaynier, George M. Campbell, Gustafson, Hemminger, Herzog, Hilbert, John J. van Buren, Kyne, Lamons, Levy, McAnn, McClelland, McConnell, Marts, Micka, Milton Lewis, Muir, Neal A. Scott, O'Neill, Osterhaus, Oswald, Parks, Pennewill, Reybold, Riddle, Rinehart, Roberts, Roche, Russell M. Cox, Samuel S. Miles, Slater, Snyder, Stern, Straub, Sutton, Swearer, Thomas, Thornhill, Tills, Trumpeter, Waterman, Weaver, Wesson, Wingfield.* Edsall class: *Blair, Brister, Brough, Calcaterra, Camp, Chambers, Chatelain, Cockrill, Dale W. Peterson, Daniel, Douglas L. Howard, Durant, Edsall, Falgout, Farguqhar, Fessenden, Finch, Fiske, Flaherty, Forster, Frederick C. Davis, Frost, Hammann, Harveson, Haverfield, Herbert C. Jones, Hill, Hissem, Holder, Howard D. Crow, Hurst, Huse, Inch, J.R.Y. Blakely, J. Richard Ward, Jacob Jones, Janssen, Joyce, Keith, Kirkpatrick, Koiner, Kretchmer, Lansing, Leopold, Lowe, Marchand, Martin H. Ray, Menges, Merrill, Mills, Moore,*

Mosley, Neunzer, Newell, O'Reilly, Otterstetter, Peterson, Pettit, Pillsburn, Poole, Pople Price, Pride, Ramsden, Rhodes, Richey, Ricketts, Robert E. Peary, Roy O. Hale, Savage, Sellstrom, Sloat, Snowden, Stanton, Stewart, Stockdale, Strickland, Sturtevant, Swasey, Swenning, Thomas L. Gary, Tomich, Vance, Wilhoite, Willis. Evarts class: *Andres, Austin, Bebas, Brackett, Brennan, Burden R. Hastings, Cabana, Canfield, Carlson, Charles R. Greer, Cloues, Connolly, Crouter, Crowley, Decker, Deede, Dempsey, Dionne, Dobler, Doherty, Donaldson, Doneff, Duffy, Edgar C. Chase, Edward C. Daly, Eisele, Elden, Emery, Engstrom, Evarts, Fair, Finnegan, Fleming, Halloran, Gilmore, Greiner, Griswold, Harold C. Thomas, Lake, Le Hardy, Lovering, Lyman, Manlove, Martin, Mitchell, Rall, Reynolds, Sanders, Sederstrom, Seid, Smartt, Stadtfeld, Steele, Tisdale, Walter S. Brown, Whitman, Wileman, William C. Millar, Wintle, Wyffels, Wyman.* John C. Butler class: *Abercrombie, Albert T. Harris, Alvin C. Cockrell, Bivin, Cecil J. Doyle, Charles E. Brannon, Chester T. O'Brien, Conklin, Corbesier, Cross, Dennis, Douglas A. Munro, Doyle C. Barnes, Dufilho, Edmonds, Edward H. Allen Edwin A. Howard, Eversole, Formoe, Francovich, French, Gentry, George E. Davis, Gilligan, Goss, Grady, Haas, Hanna, Henry W. Tucker, Heyliger, Howard F. Clark, Jaccard, Jack Miller, Jesse Rutherford, John C. Butler, John L. Williamson, Johnnie Hutchins, Joseph E. Connolly, Kendall C. Campbell, Kenneth M. Willett, Keppler, Key, Kleinsmith, La Prade, Lawrence C. Taylor, Le Ray Wilson, Leland E. Thomas, Lewis, Lloyd E. Acree, Lloyd Thomas, McCoy Reynolds, McGinty, Mack, Maurice J. Manuel, Melvin R. Nawman, Naifeh, O'Flaherty, Oberrender, Oliver Mitchell, Osberg, Pratt, Presley, Raymond, Richard M. Rowell, Richard S. Bull, Richard W. Suesens, Rizzi, Robert Brazier, Robert F. Keller, Rolf, Rombach, Samuel B. Roberts, Shelton, Silverstein, Stafford, Steinaker, Straus, Tabberer, Thaddeus Parker, Traw, Tweedy, Tulvert M. Moore, Vandivier, Wagner, Walter C. Wann, Walton, Weiss, William C. Lawe, William Sieverling, Williams, Woodrow R. Thompson, Woodson.* Rudderrow class: *Bray, Chaffee, Charles J. Kimmel, Coates, Daniel A. Joy, Day, DeLong, Eugene E. Elmore, George A. Johnson, Hodges, Holt, Jobb, Leslie L.B. Knox, Lough, McNulty, McTivier, Parle, Peiffer, Riley Rudderow, Thomas F. Nickel, Tinsman.*
Page 58 Dealey/Courtney/Claud Jones class: *Bauer, Bridget, Charles Berry, Claud Jones, Courtney, Cromwell, Dealey, Evans, Hammerberg, Hartley, Hooper, J.K. Taussig, John R. Perry, John Willis, Lester, McMorris, Van Voorhis.*
Page 59 Bronstein class: *Bronstein, McCloy.*
Garcia class: *Albert David, Bradley, Brumby, Davidson, Edward McDonnell, Garcia, Koelsch, O'Callaghan Sample, Voge.* Brooke class: *Brooke, Julius A. Furer, Ramsey, Richard L. Page, Schofield, Talbot.*
Page 60 Knox class: *Ainsworth, Aylwin, Badger, Bagley, Barbey, Blakeley, Bowen, Brewton, Capodanno, Connole, Cook, Donald B. Beary, Downes, Elmer Montgomery, Fanning,*

Franic Hammon, Gray, Harold E. Holt, Hepburn, Jesse L. Brown, Joseph Hewes, Kirk, Knox, Lang, Lockwood, McCandless, Marvin Shields, Meyercord, Miller, Moinester, Ouellet, Patterson, Paul, Pharris, Rathburne, Reasoner, Roark, Robert E. Peary, Stein, Thomas C. Hart, Trippe, Truett, Valdez, Vreeland, W.S. Sims, Whipple.

Page 61 Oliver Hazard Perry class: *Antrim, Aubrey, Fitch, Boone, Carr, Clark, Clifton Sprague, Copeland, Crommelin, Curts, De Wert, Doyle, Duncan, Elrod, Estocin, Fahrion, Flatley, Ford, Gallery, Gary, George Philip, Halyburton, Hawes, Ingraham, Jack Williams, Jarrett, John A. Moore, John L. Hall, Kauffman, Klakring, Lewis B. Puller, McCluskey, McInerney, Mahlon S. Tisdale, Nicholas, Oliver Hazard Perry, Reid, Rentz, Reuben James, Robert G. Bradley, Rodney M. Davis, Samuel B. Roberts, Samuel Eliot Morison, Sides, Simpson, Stark, Stephen W. Groves, Taylor, Thach, Underwood, Vandegrift, Wadsworth.*

Page 62 Spica class: *Airone, Alcione, Aldebaran, Altair Andromeda, Antares, Aretusa, Ariel, Calipso, Calliope, Canopo, Cassiopea, Castore, Centauro, Cigno, Circe, Climene, Clio, Libra, Lince, Lira, Lupo, Pallade, Partenope, Perseo, Pleiadi, Polluce, Sagittario, Sirio, Vega.*

Page 63 Ariete class: *Alabarde, Ariete, Arturo, Auriga, Balestra, Daga, Dragone, Eridano, Fionda, Gladio, Lancia, Pugnale, Rigel, Spada, Spica, Stella Polare.*

Page 64 Pegaso class: *Orione, Orsa, Pegaso, Procione.* Ciclone class: *Aliseo, Animoso, Ardente, Ardimentoso, Ardito, Ciclone, Fortunale, Ghibli, Groppo, Impavido, Impetuoso, Indomito, Intrepido, Monsone, Tifone, Uragano.*

Page 65 Albatros class: *Airone, Albatros, Alcione, Aquila.* De Cristofaro class: *Licio Visintini, Pietro de Cristofaro, Salvatore Todaro, Umberto Grosso.*

Page 66 Centauro class: *Canopo Centauro, Cigno, Castore.*

Page 67 Bergamini class: *Carlo Margottini, Luigi Rizzo, Virginio Fasan.* Alpini class: *Alpini, Carabiniere.*

Page 68 Lupo class: *Lupo, Orsa, Perseo, Sagittario.* Artigliere class: *Artigliere, Aviere, Bersagliere, Granatiere.*

Page 69 Maestrale class: *Aliseo, Espero, Euro, Grecale, Libeccio, Maestrale, Scirocco, Zeffiro.*

Page 70 Minerva class: *Chimera, Danaide, Driade, Fenice, Minerva, Sfinge, Sibilla, Urania.*

Page 71 Kola class: Names uncertain.

Page 72 Riga class: Known names: *Astrakhan'skiy Komsomolets, Arkhangel'skiy, Komsomolets, Bars, Barsuk, Bobr, Buyvol, Byk, Gepard, Giena, Komsomolets Litviy, Krasnogarskiy, Komsomolets, Kunitsa, Leopard, Lev, Lisa, Medved, Pantera, Rys, Rosomakha, Shakal, Sovetskiy, Azerbaydzhan, Sovetskiy, Dagestan, Sovetskiy Turkmenistan, Strau, Tigr, Tuman, Volk, Voron, Yaguar.*

Page 73 Petya and Mirka classes: Names unconfirmed.

Page 74 Poti class: Names unconfirmed.

Page 75 Grisha classes: Names unconfirmed.

Page 76 Krivak I class: *Bditel'nyi, Bezukoriznennyy, Bezzavetnyy, Bodryy, Deyatel'nyy, Doblestnyy, Dostonyy, Druzhnyy, Ladnyy, Leningradski Komsomolets, Letuchiy, Poryvistyy, Pylkiy, Razumnyy, Razayshchiy, Restivyy, Sil'nyy, Storozhevoy, Svirepyy, Zadornyy, Zharkyy.* Krivak class II: *Bessmennyy, Gordelivyy, Gromkiy, Grozyashchiy, Neukrotimyy, Pytlivyy, Razitel'nyy, Revnostnyy, Rezkiy, Rezvyy, Ryanyy.* Krivak class III: *Anadyr, Dzerzhinskiy, Kedrov, Menzhinskiy, Orel, Pskov, Vorovskiy.*

Page 77 Steregushchiy class: *Boiky, Soobrziltel'nyy, Steregushchiy, Stoiky.*

Page 78 Köln class: *Augsburg, Braunschweig, Emden, Karlsruhe, Köln, Lübeck.*

Page 79 Thetis class: *Hermes, Naiade, Theseus, Thetis, Triton.*

Page 80 Bremen class: *Augsberg, Bremen, Emden, Karlsruhe, Köln Lübeck, Niedersachsen, Rheinland-Pfalz.*

Page 81 Brandenburg class: *Bayern, Brandenburg, Mecklesnburg-Vorpommern, Schleswig-Holstein.*

Page 82 Sachsen class: *Hamburg, Hessen, Sachsen.*

Page 83 Braunschweig class: *Braunschweig, Erfurt, Magdeburg, Oldenburg.*

Page 84 Van Heemskerck class: *Jacob van Heemskerck, Witte de With.* Kortenaer class: *Abraham Crijnssen, Banckert, Bloys van Treslong, Callenburgh, Jan van Brakel, Kortenaer, Philips van Almonde, Piet Heyn, Pieter, Florisz, Van Kinsbergen.*

Page 85 De Zeven Provinciën class: *De Ruyter, De Zeven Provinciën, Evertsen, Tromp.*

Page 86 Karel Doorman class: *Abraham van der Hulst, Karel Doorman, Van Amstel, Van Galen, Van Nes, Van Speijk.*

Page 87 St. Laurent classes, Annapolis type: *Annapolis, Nipigon.* Mackenzie type: *Mackenzie, Qu'appelle, Saskatchewan, Yukon.* Restigouche type: *Chaudière, Columbia, St. Croix.* Improved Restigouche type: *Gatineau, Kootenay, Restigouche, Terra Nova.* St. Laurent type: *Assiniboine, Fraser, Margaree, Ottawa, Saguenay, Skeena.*

Page 88 Iroquois class: *Algonquin, Athabaskan, Huron, Iroquois.* Halifax class: *Calgary, Charlottetown, Fredericton, Halifax, Montreal, Ottawa, Regina, St. John's, Toronto, Vancouver, Ville de Quebec, Winnepeg.*

Page 89 Anzac class (Australia): *Anzac, Arunta, Ballarat, Parramatta, Perth, Stuart, Toowoomba, Warramunga.* Anzac class (New Zealand): *Te Kaha, Te Mana.*

ABOVE: **Anzac, Anzac class.**

Glossary

AA(W) Anti-Aircraft (Warfare).

AS Anti-Submarine.

Asdic Early British term for Sonar.

ASROC Anti-Submarine Rocket. American stand-off weapon.

AS(W) Anti-Submarine (Warfare).

bhp Brake horsepower. The power output of a (usually) internal combustion engine.

calibre Bore diameter of a gun barrel. Also measure of barrel length, e.g. a 3in 70 will be of 3 x 70 = 210in length.

C-in-C Commander-in-Chief.

CIWS Close-In Weapons System. Self-contained, fully-automatic, "last-ditch" defensive system, typically comprising several high rate-of-fire cannon and/or short-range SAMs.

CODAG Combined Diesel And Gas.

CODOG Combined Diesel Or Gas.

COGAG Combined Gas And Gas.

COGOG Combined Gas Or Gas.

COSAG Combined Steam And Gas.

contra-rotating propellers Propellers, as in a torpedo, mounted on coaxial shafts and rotated in opposite directions to nullify side forces.

DASH Drone Anti-Submarine Helicopter.

DDG Guided Missile Destroyer.

DDK General Purpose Destroyer.

dipping sonar Small sonar lowered by cable from a hovering helicopter. Sometimes "dunking sonar".

displacement (fl) Full load, or deep, displacement of a ship which is fully equipped, stored and fuelled.

displacement (std) Standard displacement. Actual weight of a ship less fuel and other deductions allowed by treaty.

Division Boat In Imperial German Navy, a larger type of Torpedo Boat, equivalent to a flotilla leader.

DP Dual-Purpose, i.e. a gun suitable for engaging both aerial or surface targets.

draught (or "draft") Mean depth of water in which a ship may float freely. In frigates particularly, mean draught (quoted) may be considerably less than that over protruding sonars.

ECM Electronic Counter Measures.

ER Extended Range.

ESM Electronic Support Measures.

flare Outward curvature or angle of hull plating.

flotilla Standard operational unit of destroyers or frigates, particularly in the Royal Navy.

FRAM Fleet Re-habilitation And Modernization. An updating programme applied to many US destroyers.

freeboard In a warship, the vertical distance between the water to any particular point on the weather deck. Unlike merchant ships, warships do not have a designated freeboard deck.

GM Guided Missile.

Grand Fleet Title carried by the British battle fleet during World War I.

gunhouse A relatively light, enclosed containment for guns, usually not extending more than one deck below. In contradistinction to a *turret*, a usually protected containment located atop a barbette or deep armoured trunk.

HA High Angle. Usually with reference to a gun's elevation.

HA/LA High Angle/Low Angle.

Hedgehog Forward-firing AS weapon of World War II, in the form of a spigot mortar projecting 12 or 24 fast-sinking bombs in an elliptical pattern.

High Sea(s) Fleet Title carried by German Battle Fleet during World War I.

horsepower Unit of power equal to 746 Watts.

Huff-Duff Popular term for HF/DF, or High Frequency Direction Finding, used by Allied AS forces to obtain bearings of a transmitting U-boat.

ihp Indicated horsepower. The power delivered by the pistons of a reciprocating steam engine.

IR Infra-Red.

LAMPS Light Airborne Multi-Purpose System.

L/B Length-to-Breadth.

length (bp) Length between perpendiculars. Customarily the distance between forward extremity of waterline at standard displacement and the forward side of the rudder post. For American warships, lengths on design waterline and between perpendiculars are synonymous.

length (oa) Length overall.

length (wl) Length on waterline at standard displacement.

Limbo British triple-barrelled AS mortar, designed to supersede Squid.

locomotive boiler Early form of boiler in which hot products of combustion were forced through tubes to heat a surrounding water mass.

MR Medium-Range.

NATO North Atlantic Treaty Organization. Effectively a counter to the Warsaw Pact.

NBCD Nuclear, Biological and Chemical Defence.

PDMS Point-Defence Missile System.

phased-array radar A radar whose beam depends not upon a rotating antenna but upon sequential switching of a matrix of fixed, radiating elements.

QF Quick-Firing. Applied to guns with "fixed" ammunition with projectile and charge combined.

SAM Surface-to-Air-Missile.

seakeeping/seakindliness/seaworthiness All applicable to a ship's ability to cope with weather conditions in discharging her functions as an efficient, but habitable, weapons platform.

sheer Curvature of deck line in fore-and-aft direction, usually upward toward either end.

shp Shaft horsepower. Power measured at point in shaft ahead of the stern gland. Does not include losses incurred in stern gland and A-bracket, if fitted.

Sonar Equipment using sound to establish range, bearing or depth of a submerged object. May be "active", i.e. emitting pulsed energy, or "passive", i.e. listening only.

spar torpedo Warhead mounted on long spar protruding ahead of a small, fast launch. Operated by ramming target.

Squid British triple-barrelled, ahead-firing AS mortar. Precursor to Limbo. Designed to supersede the Hedgehog but not adopted by the US Navy.

SSM Surface-to-Surface Missile.

stability range The range through which a ship may list while still maintaining a positive righting moment. If exceeded, capsize will follow.

superimposition If a gun is "superimposed" on another, i.e. located at a higher level, it is said to "superfire" it.

TBD Torpedo Boat Destroyer.

tender Tending to be "crank", but not so extreme.

ton As an imperial unit of weight, equal to 2,240lb.

towed array Sonar, typically passive, taking the form of a streamed neutrally buoyant hose containing multiple hydrophones and their cabling. The length of the array permits a reasonable bearing to be established on a noise source.

trim Amount by which a ship deviates, in the fore-and-aft axis, from her designed draught.

VDS Variable Depth Sonar.

VLS Vertical Launch System.

Warsaw Pact Defunct Eastern military bloc, essentially a counter to NATO.

water-tube boiler Boiler in which water is carried in tubes surrounded by hot products of combustion. Effectively a reverse, and more efficient, concept to that of the earlier Locomotive Boiler.

Weapon "Able" (Alfa) US Navy's post-war successor to Hedgehog. Trainable stabilized mounting to fire 12 rounds per minute.

Index

ABOVE: *Mohammed V*, Floréal class.

ABOVE: **Abraham van der Hulst, Karel Doorman class.**